Aries
1988

Aries
1988

Teri King's complete horoscope
for all those whose birthdays fall between
21 March and 20 April

Pan Astral
London and Sydney

First published 1987 by Pan Books Ltd,
Cavaye Place, London SW10 9PG
© Teri King 1987
ISBN 0 330 29833 X

Typeset by Input Typesetting Ltd, London SW19 8DR
Printed and bound in Great Britain by
Cox & Wyman Ltd, Reading, Berks.

Contents

Introduction

Astrology is a very complex science. Whilst it can be useful in assessing the different aspects of human relationships, there are many misconceptions associated with it. Not the least of these is the cynic's question: 'How can zodiac forecasts be accurate for all the millions of people born under any one sign?' The answer is that all horoscopes published in newspapers, books and magazines are, of necessity, of a general nature. Unless an astrologer can work from the date, time and place of your birth, the reading given will only be true to the broadly typical member of your sign.

Take a person born on 1 May. This person is principally a subject of Taurus, simply because the Sun, ruler of willpower and feelings, occupies that portion of the heavens known as Taurus during the period 21 April to 21 May. However, there are other influences to be taken into account, for instance the Moon: this planet, ruler of the subconscious, enters a fresh sign every forty-eight hours. On the birth date in question it may have been in, say, Virgo – and if that were the case it would make this particular subject a Taurean/Virgoan. Then again the rising sign or Ascendant must also be taken into consideration. This also changes constantly, as approximately every two hours a new sign passes over the horizon. The rising sign is of utmost importance, determining the image projected by the subject to the outside world – in effect, the personality. (This is why the time of birth is essential for compiling a natal chart.) Let us suppose that in this particular instance Taurus was rising at the time of birth; this would make the individual a Taurean/Virgoan/Taurean. Now, because two of the three main influences are Taurus, the subject would be a fairly typical Taurean, displaying the faults and attributes associated with this sign. But if the Moon and the Ascendant were, say, in Aquarius, the subject would portray more the vices and virtues of a true Aquarian.

Throughout the nine planets this procedure is carried on, each making up a significant part of the subject's character; their positions, the signs they occupy, and the aspects formed from one to another all play a part in the make-up. The calculation and interpretation of these movements, the work of the astrologer, will produce an individual's birth chart. Because the heavens are constantly changing, people with identical birth charts are a very rare occurrence, although it could happen with people born at the same time and in the same place. In such a case the deciding factors as to how those individuals differ in their lives, loves, careers, financial prospects and so on would be due to environmental and parental influences.

Returning to the hypothetical Taurean: as has been said he would believe himself typical of the sign; but were the Moon and the Ascendant in the alternative positions stated he would be an Aquarian. So he would get a more dependable reading from the general Aquarian predictions than from the Taurean ones. This explains why some people swear by their newspaper horoscopes, their 'stars', while others can never believe them. But whatever his Moon sign and Ascendant, the Taurean will always display certain characteristics of his birth sign, because of the Sun's influence.

Belief in astrology does not necessarily mean believing we lead totally determined lives, that we are 'fated', or that we have no control over our destiny. What it shows is that our lives run in cycles, for good and for bad; knowing this, with the help of astrology we can make the most of, or minimize, certain patterns and tendencies. How this is done is entirely up to the individual.

For instance, if you know beforehand that you have a lucky period ahead, you can make the most of it by pushing ahead with plans and aspirations – anything that is dear to you. It follows that you can also restrain times of illness, misfortune, romantic upsets and everyday adversities.

Astrology should be used as it was originally intended – as a guide, especially to character. Throughout the ages there has never been found a better guide to character analysis, enabling people to learn and use advantageously the information relating to personality, friendship, work and romance.

Once this invaluable information has been understood it makes it easier for us to see ourselves as we really are and, what's more, as others see us. We can accept our own weaknesses and limitations and those of others. We can evolve from there to inner peace and outer confidence.

In the following pages you will find character guides, both

'positive' and 'negative', a health guide, how children can be helped by the use of astrology, your prospects in partnership and romance. Used wisely, astrology can help you through life. It is not a substitute to encourage complacency, since in the final analysis it all comes down to you. Allow astrology to walk hand in hand with you and success and happiness are virtually guaranteed.

Teri King

General Analysis

Positive characteristics

According to astrology, and by virtue of the fact that Mars is its ruler, the Aries subjects have drive, enthusiasm, enterprise and are known as pioneering individuals. Progress appeals to them and they will always go along with new ideas. The positive Aries can be an inspiration to others due to enthusiasm and an aura of go-getting ambition. Energy and ambition are often boundless in this particular character and, provided these qualities are used wisely and to their utmost, the Arien will usually go far.

The positive Arien subject will dress to impress, being very particular about appearance and wardrobe. Although the wardrobe may be inadequate the turn-out is meticulous, always neat and fresh, for Aries people recognize the fact that a good appearance lends an air of authority.

Preferring work that will offer opportunities of leadership, enjoying overcoming difficulties, Ariens will go out of their way to accept challenging situations. However, they have a happy knack of forgetting past mistakes and failures, but this ability adds to endurance in times of pressure and stress.

Ariens are impulsive, frequently finding themselves in situations that could have been avoided with a little forethought and planning. Many of their problems could be avoided, in fact, if they guarded against being too ardent, passionate and sometimes selfish.

Negative characteristics

This type has a few problems to contend with, not the least of which is an excess of the qualities associated with this sign. However, hope and boundless enthusiasm are generally replaced by recklessness and a tendency to be fickle in all matters. Nothing attempted is ever seen through to a conclusion, and activities that require tact and forethought are taken at such speed that failure is often the result. The aptitude for forgetting about past mistakes is magnified in this type and so failures will be repeated over and over again.

Unlike the positive type, this character will throw in the towel whenever a situation or project gets tough; this is his or her way of solving problems. Never taken into consideration is the fact that this sort of behaviour not only harms the Arien but also other innocent individuals.

Loyalty to others is not even considered; this quality is an undeveloped part of the character, therefore this type is not to be trusted.

What Makes Ariens Happy?

Ariens are happy when starting anything new – be it a job, a car, a fresh writing-pad or climbing into a strange bed! They are also pleased when purchasing new status symbols for themselves or when winning a game – be it tennis, Monopoly or tiddly-winks – although in actual fact there is no such thing as a 'game' to them, for it is a life and death struggle each time.

They are content when being efficiently waited upon either at home or outside, when returning a faulty purchase or reprimanding an inefficient public servant. Above all, Ariens are most happy when they know they are *the* most important person in someone else's life.

What Makes Ariens Unhappy?

They are unhappy if when in public they stain the front of a new outfit; when they are ignored; when they fail to make that million by a certain age; when they are *not* the cleverest in their family; when they have been in the sun too long (roughly ten minutes). Missing out on promotion makes them miserable, also when they are expected to attend a gathering for their in-laws and when their children don't get straight A grades or win the 100-yds dash just as they did. More unhappiness is caused if they are asked to recall past mistakes or expected to plan further ahead than tomorrow; also if someone else ends a love affair – and in general, whenever they feel inadequate in any way at all.

Partnerships

Aries Woman

With Aries Man   (21 March to 20 April)

The Arien male is renowned for literally sweeping a woman off her feet. This doesn't only happen at the beginning of the relationship, for all the way through he is subject to acts of impetuosity. The relationship may not, however, last for too long for the 'me first' attitude doesn't bode too well for partnership affairs.

He can also be quite critical and is liable to argue quite fiercely if things are not to his liking. Miss Aries, also a firebrand, will argue quite readily and this is the trade mark of an Aries/Aries relationship.

Both Ariens are attracted to get-rich-quick schemes and the financial side to the relationship may become sadly neglected with certain unfortunate results.

This relationship is likely to be a quick, fiery thing, burning itself out just as suddenly as it began. It can, however, be made to work as long as both parties recognize their own and their partner's faults.

With Taurus Man   (21 April to 21 May)

The male bull is known for his conservative outlook and steady, plodding nature. He is also decidedly set in his ways and can rarely be moved from his chosen course through life. Miss Aries, in this relationship, could soon find herself frustrated, bored and longing for more excitement. She will not be able to understand his need for mulling over decisions instead of jumping into things feet first.

The Taurus man has an artistic turn of mind, however well hidden it may be, and this is quite important to him. There is also a romantic side to his nature which needs expression constantly but, whilst trying to share these feelings with her, he may be frustrated in his attempts to get her to show any interest in his pursuits. He also demands total fidelity, both physically and emotionally; his woman belongs to HIM – no one else, and

14

he may demand more than she is able or prepared to give. This is not, as you can see, the most ideal of matches.

With Gemini Man   (22 May to 21 June)
By virtue of his irrepressible nature Mr Gemini could be something of a mystery to Miss Aries. She will be totally thrown by his tendency to be exalted one moment and in the depths of despair the next. This good-looking, sociable type may initially attract her, but in the end she could lose him through her desire to be the dominant partner. This he will rebel against, not waiting around for the result of such a battle. He may return at a later date but only if he is certain that he will not be pushed around again. The Gemini man needs to be mentally stimulated constantly and, although the Arien may want to look after him and get him to be more sensible, she will not be able to provide the stimulation needed.

Affairs with Gemini men could end quite suddenly when she finds she has a totally bored individual on her hands. She will need to develop her imagination if she wants to hang on to the Gemini man.

With Cancer Man   (22 June to 22 July)
Miss Aries could find this character a bit difficult to communicate with as he is surrounded by a defensive shell. This is put up to protect his inner, hypersensitive self. He is the type who is easily hurt but tries to appear tougher than he really is. Miss Aries, in no need of protection, will find his protective nature somewhat frustrating. If she lets this be known Mr Cancer will go off in a sulk that could last for days. The more she tries to draw him from his shell the deeper he will dig himself in.

The Cancer type is known for his tenacity, his Crab's claw clutching all that is dear to him, never letting go. His pursuits – books, music, and so on – will become as rivals to her, for generally she has no time for such things. His romantic streak will also be alien to her and he is in for a hard time trying to stimulate her in this way.

With Leo Man   (23 July to 23 August)
This relationship could start off as a fiery, passionate affair but degenerate into the doldrums due to the Leo characteristic of demanding constant admiration. Miss Aries is not the most demonstrative of types and will resent the fact that he needs,

15

always, to be the king of their particular castle. Leo has a love of flattery, he feeds on it from all sides, but this could be his downfall in a relationship with an Arien. Miss Aries will not take too kindly to other women pouring adulation upon her Leo's shoulders. However, if she can recognize that this is an integral part of his nature she may just try to remedy the situation by supplying such flattery herself; she will have to aim at being his number one admirer.

He can handle her necessity for constant change and her attraction to new and stimulating ideas. The relationship could work if both are prepared to make the necessary effort.

With Virgo Man   (24 August to 23 September)

Where Miss Aries is a woman of action, Mr Virgo is a creature of devotion and chastity, quite modest in his behaviour. A thinker. Virgo can be somewhat self-centred, as can Aries, and this lack of sharing could lead to an early rift in the partnership. Each will soon find a way of putting down suggestions and ideas raised by the other, and this will become their main platform for argument.

Finances could also lead to friction for Virgo is very careful, sometimes even stingy, with his hard-earned money. She, on the other hand, is quite a free spender, and this will not go down too well with him. The relationship is hardly likely to build on the physical side of love; she is a sexual lady, he is a mental man. Yet another area of disagreement.

With Libra Man   (24 September to 23 October)

The Aries tendency to argument could lead to an early break-up here. Libra is a harmonious creature, one who abhors any form of violence, either verbal or physical. In fact, any discordant atmosphere or surrounding will make him cringe and walk away. He loves things beautiful, has a preference for living life to the full, is very attractive to the opposite sex and conscious of his own personal magnetism. She should never take too seriously his declarations of undying love, for he is just as likely to make the same declarations to another girl later in the same week! This behaviour pattern will, undoubtedly, be too much for the Arien who will resort to argument and aggression. This is the kiss of death relationship.

With Scorpio Man   (24 October to 22 November)
The Scorpio man is renowned for his jealousy, his fixed opinions (that cannot be changed, even by Miss Aries) and his loyalty. Whilst Aries may be strong enough to resist attempts at taking her over completely she is quite likely to go against his wishes just for the sake of awkwardness. The Scorpio man will bring out the fighting side of her personality, the jealousy in his character. If she fails him in any way, especially in his set ideals which he sets for her to attain, he will push her out of his life.

She must provide a home for him where he can relax completely and cut off the rest of the outside world; this is most important to him. However, she may just find this behaviour a little too claustrophobic for her own good. It will then be she who walks out, much to his surprise.

With Sagittarius Man   (23 November to 21 December)
This could be one of the best partnerships for Miss Aries to enter into, provided that she can learn to live with his ideas on freedom, can overcome her feelings of jealousy and ignore this man's totally harmless flirtations. Also, she will have to learn to live with his ability to change his life at the drop of a hat. He is capable of changing everything at a moment's notice, including his job and environment. However, should any of his ideas collapse and fall about his ears she will be the one to pick up the pieces and put him back together again, meantime supporting him financially and emotionally until the repair job is complete.

Whilst Miss Aries is the enterprising type she could, after some time, become quite apprehensive when his next crazy inspiration falls upon her ears. Life, with him, will certainly be chaotic, but never humdrum.

With Capricorn Man   (22 December to 20 January)
Whilst going through one of her more practical moods it is quite likely that Miss Aries will become attracted to this ambitious, strong, independence-loving individual. Later, however, she will grow to resent the amount of time spent upon his career as she feels, quite rightly, that life holds more than a constant involvement in career matters.

On the other hand, this simple man could be overwhelmed by the go-getting Arien woman. Her carefree gambling nature will offend his strict code of common sense. His pessimistic

17

moods of depression will do little to cement the relationship or help to drive it forward to happiness, as he tends to throw a wet blanket over all her enthusiastic ideas.

If it were possible for these two to accept each other's faults, the union could work, but it is unlikely.

With Aquarius Man   (21 January to 19 February)
Miss Aries could find herself on the receiving end of the Aquarian man's need to change everything. He is a reformer, the type who feels a need to alter practically all he comes into contact with, be it his home, his office, his friends – the entire world. However, whilst all this change is going on it is rare that the Aquarian ever improves anything. He knows what needs to be done, but cannot always find the help necessary to carry things through. Miss Aries will have to be a friend to this man as well as a lover. She also prefers more sophisticated individuals peopling her world and will find it hard to come to terms with the eccentric types introduced to her by the Aquarian. The Aquarian is also known for his detached attitude to the people in his life, even to those whom he loves. She may be hurt when he is in one of these moods.

With Pisces Man   (20 February to 20 March)
This relationship, to say the least, could become quite complex. The Piscean man, whilst being a lovable creature, needs her Arien strength and comfort when his plans fall by the wayside. Initially his willingness to become involved in her ventures and ideas could be the attraction. However, she will not be able to manage him on the days when he slips away into his own secret, hermit-like world, whilst he is trying to come to grips with some problem or other. Pisces is not known for his decision making and will quite readily allow her to make all the important judgements. However, should they interfere with his plans he will totally ignore them.

Because the Piscean lacks any desire to change her to his way of thinking, Miss Aries could, quite conceivably, decide that this is just the man for her.

Aries Man

With Aries Woman   (21 March to 20 April)

Miss Aries is quite likely to be swept off her feet by this male counterpart, for he is known for his impulsive behaviour. The similarities in their make-up will lead to quite a fiercely passionate affair. However, the trade mark of this relationship will be argument, for both like to put themselves first. Both are attracted to get-rich-quick schemes. Money matters will be ignored and it will not be long before the relationship runs into financial difficulty. Both are quite extravagant and money will go out as soon as it comes in, if not before.

This relationship will burn itself out as quickly as it caught fire, although if both work at the union it could last – for a while.

With Taurus Woman   (21 April to 21 May)

This could be a difficult partnership to keep going, owing to both personalities' inclinations towards selfishness. He will not be dominated or pressurized in any way, and if she tries she will find that his strength of character will more than match her own. Neither has a well-developed sense of 'give and take'. She goes into a venture and always sees it through to a natural conclusion – not so the Aries. He is quite likely to get sidetracked halfway through, jumping on to some other bandwagon he thinks stands more chance of success. Whilst she is not really a stick-in-the-mud she does like familiar surroundings and this will clash quite violently with his need for change.

With Gemini Woman   (22 May to 21 June)

The strength of character, independence, confidence and general enterprise of the Arien man could, initially, impress Miss Gemini, for his decisive manner in love and business will be an attraction. Always on the search for a new or novel experience Miss Gemini will find the Aries assumption as leader in the relationship appealing to begin with. However, when she discovers that this is for real – she will quickly become bored. They will not have many interests in common, she taking no interest in his love of sport nor he in her enthusiasiam for artistic pursuits.

However, arguments will quickly be forgotten as both parties have short memories, though he is likely to recover a lot quicker than she. He is a passionate creature and his moods of affection

19

could be too much for the Gemini who will become detached and cold. She can easily cope with him, but he will find her almost impossible to understand as she is far too complex a creature.

With Cancer Woman   (22 June to 22 July)
Home-loving Cancer could quite easily be overwhelmed by this personality in the first stages of romance, so that before she knows what has happened she is too deeply involved to get out. However, it will not be that long before she realizes just how different are their aims in life. Aries is always on the search for fresh scope and activity, whilst Miss Cancer desires a quiet home life and peaceful existence.

His passions burn too fiercely for her and she will begin to suspect how long they will last. Feminine moods, especially Cancer's, leave him baffled; therefore he makes no attempt to understand them. At this point she will decide that her thoughts on love differ from his, and they will go their separate ways.

With Leo Woman   (23 July to 23 August)
Leo will be attracted to the Aries confidence, his constant involvement in the fight with life and his go-ahead enterprise. However, she will soon begin to worry about his impulsive nature. Leo prefers to consider all angles of a situation before acting. Their egos are a match for each other – both being sensitive, needing admiration and encouragement. Fierce quarrels could arise if either ego is bruised by the other. Life will then deteriorate into a constant battle for supremacy. If she wishes the relationship to last she should allow him to win at least a few of their battles, for they both thrive on argument and a certain amount of conflict. Leo's ambitions, should they become more important than his own, will again lead to conflict and an eventual split in the partnership.

With Virgo Woman   (24 August to 23 September)
This pair look at life from totally different viewpoints. He lives in the past, she in the future. Financial matters will cause the Arien no concern, whilst she will be constantly planning ahead, never assuming that *something* will turn up. Here they can find each other totally incompatible. Their working lives also differ; he is only interested in working hard when his imagination has been fired with enthusiasm, and this usually leads to many

different occupations; she prefers to have a steady job offering security and little risk, an attitude he abhors.

Virgo is known as a nagging individual who uses her sharp tongue as a weapon. This behaviour is likely to cause Aries some amusement – until he has had enough of it. He is then likely to move straight on to another, more agreeable partner. Virgo should try to make her own personality more adaptable if she wishes the partnership to survive.

With Libra Woman   (24 September to 23 October)

Somehow the attraction of these two is often strong, probably because the Libran woman is so attractive to the opposite sex. However, it hardly ever lasts. There has to be an equality in all her relationships with the opposite sex, and his efforts to be the dominant partner will, at first, amuse her. Later she will be horrified when she realizes that he is very serious in his intentions. Libra has a natural gift for self-expression; Aries finds difficulty expressing himself most of the time. This leads to frustration on her part and a belief that her verbal endearments are a sign of weakness. They both have impulsive natures, another reason why the attraction started in the first place. There is no sentiment in the Arien make-up and this will upset the Libran lady, she likes to look back over a relationship and base her plans for the future upon it. Here the Aries will refuse to cooperate, as with her attitude towards helping others. He is too selfish, whilst she is a giving, sharing person.

With Scorpio Woman   (24 October to 22 November)

The emphasis in this relationship will be that of conflict and war. The Scorpio woman is, like Aries, a born fighter and this tendency will eventually undermine the relationship, rather than protecting it against outsiders. Scorpio is very fixed in her opinions and ideals and refuses to accept the fact that she may sometimes be wrong. This will not please Aries for he is willing to listen, at least, to another point of view. Miss Scorpio is a fiercely emotional creature, but Aries dispenses with emotion wherever possible believing that it restricts the individual. Therefore her emotional ravings will certainly end in a fight for he believes them to be neurotic and quite unnecessary. These two will find it very difficult to be friends – let alone anything of a more emotional significance.

With Sagittarius Woman   (23 November to 21 December)

This could be an instant attraction, for the strength and warmth of Aries will instantly appeal. However, she will soon find out about his desire to dominate and possess her. Meanwhile she may well cool her emotions whilst trying to decide whether or not she can accept this state of affairs. She will probably decide that, just this once, she can allow herself to be tied to someone else. She will offer enthusiasm whenever he comes to her with new ideas on how to raise money, improve living conditions, and so on. No matter how wild these schemes may be she will always be there, up front with him. She is good for an ego boost when his spirits are flagging after yet another failure. Aries is not known for his perseverance with ideas. But Sagittarius is hopelessly impractical when it comes to finance and, possibly for the first time, he will have to find the necessary responsibility to manage their affairs. Normally this is a very happy relationship.

With Capricorn Woman   (22 December to 20 January)

This lady will, no doubt, be knocked over sideways by Aries' protestations of undying love, and allow herself to fall in love with his strong character. Later she will realize her mistake. The very first time one of his schemes comes to naught, or he doesn't see it through to a conclusion, she will be disillusioned and somewhat insecure in his company. She likes security, has an abhorrence of debt and believes her man should work stoically towards an objective. Get-rich-quick schemes will not appeal to her. She is unlikely ever to adapt to his way of life – constantly changing jobs, chasing dreams and challenges – and in time he will seek encouragement elsewhere. Capricorn is a social animal, and the saving grace in this relationship could be brought about by the Arien social scene. However, put a man in the room with Capricorn and she will immediately respond – this will upset Aries who is extremely possessive. Jealousy will rear its head and cause the final rift.

With Aquarius Woman   (21 January to 19 February)

This woman, constantly surrounded by others in active debate, will attract Aries who likes activity of any description. Later he will find that her interest in others does not extend to him and as he is basically a self-centred person this attitude will be the basis for many an argument. Should she attack his sensitive ego, all the force of his fiery temper will be directed at her. The Aquarian likes all relationships to be based on friendship. This is impossible for the Aries to accept, for he finds it impossible to make friends with those other than his own sex. Being a born leader he will resent the fact that Miss Aquarius has every intention of following a career of her own. This will be further aggravated by the Arien possessive streak which makes him very reluctant to allow her to be involved in any task that does not include him.

With Pisces Woman   (20 February to 20 March)

Miss Pisces is an intuitive creature and, despite Aries's declarations of love, she will sense that her personal freedom and identity are about to be overwhelmed. She will find that he fully intends to use her femininity and adaptable character in order to bend her to his way of life. Her strange, changeable moods will not be fully understood, but this will not perturb him too much as he will attach little importance to them. This attitude will soon get on her nerves, and she will know that a full understanding can never be reached.

Her own career will rate no attention from him and is quite likely to slide into the background, taking second place to everything he does. He will expect her support in all his own ventures, no matter how futile they turn out to be. The strain of this will be too much for such a feminine creature. Finances could become chaotic if he foolishly believes he can leave that side of things to her for she is hopeless when it comes to monetary matters and the pressure of this responsibility could make her physically ill. However, this relationship, given a bit of 'give and take', could succeed, but it is unlikely, for Aries does not know the meaning of the phrase.

Romantic Prospects 1988

Have you ever wondered why suddenly for no apparent reason you lose interest in love and in sex? No? Don't pretend that it never happens to you. Let me refresh that grey matter.

There you are after a couple of sexually, or romantically, hectic weeks considering applying for the lover-of-the-year award when, quite suddenly, the TV becomes more attractive than any member of the opposite sex you have seen for some time. Could it be connected with your birth sign? Yes, it most certainly can. Venus and Mars are the planets that count.

Favourably placed, they improve your looks, vitality and zest for living, but when they gang up on you, you have about as much confidence in yourself as King Kong at a beauty contest! Your nerves jangle and, mentally, you are preoccupied with external matters. But not to worry, your sex appeal will return. It is simply a matter of time. The table opposite has been compiled in order to prepare you for your romantically active periods.

How to interpret the table

1 HEART – poor. If you try hard, someone of the opposite sex may decide to go out with you, but it is going to be hard work.
2 HEARTS – fair. If your lover has nothing better to do then you may be lucky, but you will need to make the move.
3 HEARTS – good. Watch out, you are getting some mighty strange looks. Whoops! Well I did warn you! It is a pretty hot time.
4 HEARTS – wow! Take cover, unless you want to be caught in the stampede.

Your Romantic Prospects for 1988

	Jan	Feb	Mar	Apr	May	June	July	Aug	Sept	Oct	Nov	Dec
Aries	♥	♥♥♥♥	♥♥	♥	♥♥	♥	♥♥	♥♥	♥♥	♥♥	♥♥♥	♥♥
Taurus	♥♥	♥	♥♥♥♥	♥♥	♥♥	♥♥	♥♥	♥♥	♥	♥♥	♥	♥♥♥
Gemini	♥	♥♥	♥♥♥♥	♥♥♥	♥♥♥♥	♥♥♥	♥♥♥	♥♥♥	♥♥	♥	♥♥♥	♥♥♥
Cancer	♥♥	♥	♥♥	♥	♥♥♥	♥	♥♥	♥♥♥	♥♥♥	♥♥	♥	♥♥
Leo	♥♥♥	♥♥♥	♥	♥	♥♥♥	♥♥	♥♥	♥♥♥	♥♥♥	♥♥	♥♥♥	♥
Virgo	♥♥♥	♥	♥♥♥	♥	♥	♥♥	♥♥	♥	♥	♥♥♥♥	♥	♥♥
Libra	♥♥	♥♥	♥	♥♥	♥♥	♥♥	♥♥	♥	♥	♥♥	♥♥♥♥	♥
Scorpio	♥♥♥	♥♥♥	♥♥♥	♥	♥	♥	♥♥♥	♥♥	♥♥	♥	♥♥	♥♥♥
Sagittarius	♥	♥♥♥	♥♥♥	♥♥♥	♥♥♥	♥♥	♥♥♥	♥	♥♥♥	♥	♥♥	♥♥♥
Capricorn	♥♥	♥	♥♥♥	♥♥	♥	♥	♥♥	♥♥♥	♥	♥	♥♥	♥♥
Aquarius	♥♥♥♥	♥♥	♥	♥♥♥	♥♥	♥	♥	♥♥	♥	♥	♥	♥♥
Pisces	♥♥♥♥♥	♥♥♥	♥	♥♥♥	♥♥	♥♥	♥♥	♥♥	♥	♥♥♥	♥	♥♥

Health Year 1988

We all have our accident-prone days. You know the kind of thing: you get out of bed and walk into the bedroom door, fall down the stairs, trip over the cat, burn your hands on the kettle and then, finally, as you rush out of the door to catch that important train you discover that it is Sunday! Does this sound familiar? Of course. There are also other days when, for no apparent reason you wake up with nerves jangling. The slightest noise, like the rustle of a newspaper, and you are reaching for the tranquillizers! Could this have anything to do with astrology? Yes.

Each physical ailment is a symptom of a bad aspect from Mars, Venus, Jupiter, etcetera. The table overleaf has been compiled in order for you to check out your bad weeks, and with any luck prepare for them.

How to interpret

THE HAMMER This is the symbol of the headache. Possibly caused by tension, toothache or simply a hangover.

THE WARNING Watch out – those nerves will be easily shredded. Put in your ear plugs and hope for the best.

BLACK CLOUD Depression. There will be a tendency for you during this week to feel that the end of the world is nigh. Take constructive steps to keep yourself occupied.

BANDAGED FINGER Accident prone. Anything from a cut finger to a sore heel.

THE APPLE Relax – you are hale and hearty.

Your Health Year 1988

	1st week	2nd week	3rd week	4th week
Jan				
Feb				
Mar				
Apr				
May				
June				
July				
Aug				
Sept				
Oct				
Nov				
Dec				

Marriage Year 1988

Marriage can be a pretty crazy business at the best of times, or should I say the worst? So, can astrology affect it? Yes. When a marriage comes under the influence of Venus, all in the Garden of Love is pink clouds and beautiful sunsets, but when Mars decides to oppose your marriage, watch out for fireworks. Getting on with your partner at this time can be something of a challenge.

The graph opposite has been compiled in order to help you through the coming year. For let us not forget, prevention is often better than cure. If you know that your spouse is going to be in a touchy mood, then you can be extra loving, if you are wise. If you are not – don't say I didn't warn you!

How to interpret

THE BALLOON Shows a week taken up with socializing which, for the most part, should be happy.

THE CLOCK Watch out for boredom. It will eat away at your relationship, not to mention your brain!

THE HEART This is fairly self-explanatory. Time for romance, soft lights, sweet music and an early night!

THE BOMB Mars is acting against you. Therefore, you can expect arguments through tension and general dissatisfaction. If you want your relationship to last, you should be patient and extra loving during these weeks.

THE DOVE A peaceful time.

Your Marriage Year 1988

	1st week	2nd week	3rd week	4th week
Jan	balloon	dove	dove	clock
Feb	clock	heart	heart	heart
Mar	heart	balloon	bomb	bomb
Apr	clock	dove	dove	balloon
May	dove	clock	balloon	balloon
June	dove	heart	dove	balloon
July	dove	clock	bomb	bomb
Aug	dove	bomb	dove	balloon
Sept	balloon	heart	heart	bomb
Oct	bomb	clock	clock	heart
Nov	heart	heart	dove	clock
Dec	clock	dove	bomb	heart

Saturn and Your Responsibilities

Are you pessimistic and prone to depression? Do you accept burdens and responsibilities willingly? Do you work harder than other people? Is your path in life rocky through no fault of your own? Saturn influences all such behaviour and situations. It is important for every adult who has encountered more than his share of obstacles to understand the position of Saturn in his own particular horoscope.

Saturn in Aries

Saturn was in Aries during the following periods:

15 December 1910 to 19 January 1911
25 April 1937 to 17 October 1937
14 January 1938 to 5 July 1939
22 September 1939 to 19 March 1940
4 March 1967 to 29 April 1969

Saturn in Aries places severe limitations on the success you can achieve in life . Although success can come to you through some activity that appeals to the public at large, it is not yours for the asking and is usually only arrived at after much turmoil and pain. Often it is denied altogether, as if fate had decreed that you would be thwarted by every conceivable obstacle and prevented from realizing your promise to the full. While many famous and successful people have this position of Saturn, most of them have experienced either disappointment and unfulfilled ambition in some way, or loss of popularity or both. Sometimes your afflictions come instead from poor health, although you may heroically try to lead a normal life despite this. Or there is some external affliction which prevents you from reaching your goal. However, you should never be defeatist but remember that it is the experiences of life which are valuable rather than the outcome, which is so often decided by forces beyond your control.

You are, nevertheless, apt to be prominent either within your own circle or in the world at large. You are sure of yourself and quite ambitious, although you have a tendency to be strict and somewhat solitary. In some cases, you may be a hermit or a recluse at heart. You may also have an inclination to be rather grumpy on social occasions and find it hard to fit in. You have more acquaintances than close friends.

When this position of Saturn really works against you, it may affect your sight or hearing. Severe headaches and trouble with the teeth are also likely.

Famous people with Saturn in Aries:

Robert Louis Stevenson	George Washington
Cecil B. DeMille	Albert Einstein
Barry Goldwater	Rudolf Nureyev
W. C. Fields	

Saturn in Taurus

Saturn was in Taurus during the following periods:

20 January 1911 to 6 July 1912
1 December 1912 to 26 March 1913
6 July 1939 to 21 September 1939
20 March 1940 to 8 May 1942
29 April 1969 to 18 June 1971
10 January 1972 to 21 February 1972

Those with Saturn in Taurus tend to be stubborn, determined and very stable. They are usually moral and have a fine sense of responsibility. They are able to surmount whatever difficulty comes their way, but their path in life is not usually strewn with insurmountable obstacles. They have firm convictions which they will fight to preserve, also the will and ability to succeed and win over any opposition. But they may not do this overnight. However, theirs is no 'flash-in-the-pan' brilliance but a patient, plodding dedication to a cause.

This is an excellent position for victory for a military person. Ulysses S. Grant, Joan of Arc and Alexander the Great all had Saturn in Taurus. The firm will and driving determination to win are not only an asset in wars, but may lead to a triumphant career in other fields. In fact, you can achieve success in any vocation where patience and perseverance are required.

However, this is not a particularly fortunate position financially. You do not make money easily, and to compensate for this

31

you tend to save the money you do get; you are not particularly generous.

The most vulnerable part of your body is the throat. This position of Saturn tends to dull somewhat the senses of taste and touch.

Famous people with Saturn in Taurus:

Louis Pasteur	Laurence Rockefeller
Igor Stravinsky	Danny Kaye
Richard Nixon	Vincent van Gogh
Joan Baez	

Saturn in Gemini

Saturn was in Gemini during the following periods:

7 July 1912 to 30 November 1912
26 March 1913 to 24 August 1914
7 December 1914 to 11 May 1915
9 May 1942 to 19 June 1944
19 June 1971 to 9 January 1972
22 February 1972 to 1 August 1973
8 January 1974 to 18 April 1974

Saturn is well-placed here. Mercury rules Gemini, and as Saturn is considered the best influence on Mercury, this can be an altogether felicitous combination of worldly wisdom and youthful intellect. It can result in a person capable of the suave sophistication of a venerable diplomat cloaked in something like a schoolboy's naivety. Saturn so placed serves to steady the mind and at the same time sharpen it and make it more versatile. There can be great success in intellectual endeavours.

Yet these people commonly experience sorrow in childhood or through relatives, or they may have difficulty in getting an education. At some time in their life, they could even be forced to live in exile. The patience and thought essential to great literary efforts is implicit in those whose Saturn is well-aspected. Their understanding is comprehensive, profound, and highly intellectual. There is a flair for finance, although they may not necessarily be clever with figures or simple arithmetic.

Saturn in Gemini can also give musical ability, to conduct, compose or sing. In art, there is a formidable mastery of line with the very great; with ordinary people, a natural ability to draw.

However, this placing tends to have an adverse effect on the chest and lungs. When badly aspected, there is also a danger in transportation by air.

Famous people with Saturn in Gemini:

Muhammad Ali	Oscar Wilde
Sigmund Freud	Willy Brandt

Saturn in Cancer

Saturn was in Cancer during the following periods:
25 August 1914 to 6 December 1914
12 May 1915 to 17 October 1916
8 December 1916 to 24 June 1917
20 June 1944 to 2 August 1946
2 August 1973 to 7 January 1974
19 April 1974 to 16 September 1975

This is not a particularly favourable position for Saturn, as it results in laxity, laziness and a tendency to over-indulge in food, drink, sex and other sensual pleasures. It does not rule out outstanding accomplishments in the professions of the artistic or business worlds, but these people are usually dissolute and intemperate when their work is through.

The stomach is the most vulnerable part of the body, as well as the breast in the case of a woman. Obesity, ulcers and obstructions or wasting diseases involving the digestion are probable, especially when Saturn is afflicted.

Often the home and mother prove a source of sorrow; perhaps you lost your mother at a very early age, or she had troubles which she shared with you or burdens she thrust upon you. Alternatively, she might have been excessively strict and a harsh disciplinarian. In any event, complexes later on in life can stem from your early relationship with your mother. In some cases your childhood home might have failed to provide you with even the most meagre comforts. For others, Saturn in Cancer could refer to adversity in the home during your declining years, or a downfall of some kind at the end of your career. If you have experienced none of these disadvantages, then for you Saturn is well-aspected.

Famous people with Saturn in Cancer:

Eugene McCarthy	Balzac
Napoleon Bonaparte	Michelangelo
Dean Martin	Mia Farrow
John F. Kennedy	

Saturn in Leo

Saturn was in Leo during the following periods:

17 October 1916 to 7 December 1916
25 June 1917 to 12 August 1919
3 August 1946 to 18 September 1948
3 April 1949 to 28 May 1949
17 September 1975 to 14 January 1976
5 June 1976 to 16 November 1977
5 January 1978 to 25 July 1978

There is little harmony between the slow, heavy, depressing Saturn and the noble, expansive Leo. This combination may give you more than your share of heartaches and disappointments. Saturn in Leo gives many frustrations and to some extent restricts your emotional responses. You are inclined to be rather cold and analytical. Your friends are usually of your own choosing: you are not particularly susceptible to the friendly advances of other people, tending to be suspicious that compliments are merely another form of flattery. Nor do you like others to openly display their affection to you.

You are often a very able diplomat, however, since you calculate every move, which can be an asset in public life or entertainment. You know exactly what to do to be popular, but Saturn in Leo may make you less warm and human than you might otherwise be. You are, however, so subtle and astute that others may not suspect the true extent of your inner reserve.

When badly aspected, Saturn in this position can cause a tragic downfall. It is unfavourable for heads of governments or military leaders. With ordinary people, it not only causes them to experience sorrow, but it also makes them heartless about inflicting unhappiness on other people.

Famous people with Saturn in Leo:

Charlie Chaplin	Adolf Hitler
Margot Fonteyn	Billy Graham
Tolstoy	

Saturn in Virgo

Saturn was in Virgo durimg the following periods:

3 August 1919 to 7 October 1921
19 September 1948 to 2 April 1949
29 May 1949 to 20 November 1950
7 March 1951 to 13 August 1951
18 November 1977 to 4 January 1978
26 July 1978 to 20 September 1980

There is much harmony between Saturn and Virgo and the effect on the mind is admirable. As in the case of Saturn in Gemini, Mercury's ruling of the sign in which Saturn is found has the effect of combining the wisdom of age with the mental vigour of youth. However, Saturn in Virgo is more earthy and more practical.

When well-aspected, this position gives the ability to understand matters which are intellectually very weighty. It also produces the power to analyse, criticize and organize which, when coupled with other good placings on the birth chart, promises leadership ability and adds mental strength and stability. In addition, there is the ability to reason in both a practical and theoretical way. The result is true wisdom; a strong sense of thought and practical judgement result from a well-aspected Saturn in Virgo.

When badly aspected, there may be some unnecessary niggling over details, or petty tyrannies. There may be a bent for agriculture and you can be possessed of a green thumb when it comes to growing things. Your farming techniques are the most effective because your approach is based on up-to-date scholarship as well as on sound instincts.

You tend to be something of a lone wolf – capable of keeping your own counsel and refreshed and nourished by your moments of solitude.

Famous people with Saturn in Virgo:

Prince Philip
Carol Channing
Prince Charles
Victor Hugo

John Glenn
Charles de Gaulle
Princess Anne

Saturn in Libra

Saturn was in Libra during the following periods:

8 October 1921 to 19 December 1923
6 April 1924 to 13 September 1924
21 November 1950 to 6 March 1951
14 August 1951 to 22 October 1953
21 September 1980 to 28 November 1982
7 May 1983 to 23 August 1983

This is a truly excellent position for Saturn. You have extraordinarily good judgement, and unless Saturn is very afflicted, you are quite capable of looking out for your own interests. You are tactful in your dealings with other people and make an astute politician as well as a just administrator. At your best, you are philosophical and wise.

You can benefit through partnership with an older person, or you may even marry someone older or more serious than yourself. You need marriage for its stabilizing influence and you are a devoted spouse unless Saturn is very afflicted – in which case you will experience sorrow in marriage or suffering through divorce.

You may be a mystic in religion, and you are truly religious in the deepest sense. Your sense of justice is highly developed and you have a deep-seated desire to be fair. Politicians with Saturn so placed are just, clever and astute.

This is a favourable influence for artistic endeavours, indicating a masterful technique and terseness of expression. There is not one superfluous detail or line to detract from the austere purity of the composition.

When Saturn is well-aspected, you save a great deal of time travelling by air. When it is afflicted, there may be either danger or discomfort in air transport.

This position may indicate some trouble with the back, or obstructions affecting the kidneys.

Famous people with Saturn in Libra:

James Arness	Judy Garland
Henri Toulouse-Lautrec	J. M. W. Turner
J. Paul Getty	Benjamin Disraeli
Oliver Cromwell	

Saturn in Scorpio

Saturn was in Scorpio during the following periods:

19 December 1923 to 5 April 1924
14 September 1924 to 2 December 1926
23 October 1953 to 12 January 1956
14 May 1956 to 10 October 1956
29 November 1982 to 6 May 1983
24 August 1983 to 16 November 1985

Saturn lends subtlety and ambition to the most passionate of all the zodiac signs. You are shrewd and astute, and you use your innate worldly wisdom to gain the material power you usually desire. Your ego is strong and you are well able to advance yourself in the course of your lifetime. Although a forceful character, you conceal your strength under a pleasant, agreeable exterior. Not only do you control and direct your own passions, but you also dominate other people. However, in private life you tend to be rather selfish and obstinate.

If Saturn is badly aspected, you are in danger of losing your reputation and becoming unpopular through scandal-mongering and character assassination.

This position is disadvantageous for health when you are young, but once that danger point is past you have a good chance of living to a ripe old age. Health difficulties promised by this position of Saturn tend to affect you through the generative organs.

You may derive much benefit from joining secret societies or mystical groups. You are naturally very secretive and are inclined to be interested in the occult.

Famous people with Saturn in Scorpio:

Doris Day	Robert F. Kennedy
Richard Burton	Dick Van Dyke
Queen Elizabeth II	Sammy Davis, Jr.
Rock Hudson	

Saturn in Sagittarius

Saturn was in Sagittarius during the following periods:

9 July 1900 to 16 October 1900
3 December 1926 to 15 March 1929

5 May 1929 to 29 November 1929
13 January 1956 to 13 May 1956
11 October 1956 to 5 January 1959
17 November 1985 to 13 February 1988

This position of Saturn does not tend towards easy success. However, success is not denied; instead it is delayed, and you may find it hard to overcome early setbacks in order to reach your goal. Perhaps it is this kind of adversity which not only teaches you the philosophy and wisdom that make your contributions so valuable later on, but also gives you your understanding of human nature and compassion for others. You are an idealist, you have vision and can show true dedication to a cause.

If Saturn is well-aspected, this is a wonderful position for ministers, lawyers, philosophers, scientists, statesmen, writers or those answering any calling requiring a knowledge of foreign affairs. Travel and occupations connected with it may be sobering experiences, but they give you a broader point of view. There is a high incidence of deaths for political reasons among public figures with this position of Saturn: Lincoln, Gandhi and Martin Luther King all died at the hands of assassins at a time when they were espousing controversial issues and defending their ideals. Their Saturn in Sagittarius, however, was to a great extent responsible for their integrity and prominence in public life.

You are naturally thrifty, and while you are generous with others you do not spend very much on yourself.

Famous people with Saturn in Sagittarius:

Fidel Castro	Thomas Hardy
Sidney Poitier	Caroline Kennedy

Saturn in Capricorn

Saturn was in Capricorn during the following periods:

21 January 1900 to 18 July 1900
17 October 1900 to 19 January 1903
16 March 1929 to 4 May 1929
30 November 1929 to 23 February 1932
13 August 1932 to 19 November 1932

6 January 1959 to 3 January 1962
12 November 1988 to 6 February 1991

Saturn in his own sign emphasizes some of the planet's less desirable traits. You may have to contend with more than your share of obstacles and hardships, but you are definitely not prepared to endure them with equanimity. Indeed, you are very determined. You want your own way and if someone denies it to you, you are apt to become enraged. In fact, from the time you were small you have been furious whenever anyone opposed you. Sometimes you are downright dictatorial. You do not have the finesse of Saturn in Libra or Sagittarius and your methods can appear rough or harsh in comparison.

However, Saturn's better qualities are also emphasized by his placing in his own sign. There is much worldly ambition and know-how. You try not to be in a position of dependence on anyone, and you have a tendency to do everything yourself – the hard way. In some cases, this is your lot through force of circumstance; in others, you have such a difficult time because you tend not to listen to those who would wish to spare you unnecessary problems. In either case, you learn by experience and when you have finished, you can stand very solidly on your own two feet.

You may have been a timid child, but as an adult you are authoritarian and a power in the world. This position indicates a certain selfishness, and loneliness is sometimes the result. However, if there are aspects to counteract this a little on your birth chart, then you may have many sterling qualities.

This position can give rheumatism in the joints, especially in the knees.

Famous people with Saturn in Capricorn:

Charles Dickens	Walt Disney
Ed Sullivan	Edward M. Kennedy
John Osborne	Princess Margaret

Saturn in Aquarius

Saturn was in Aquarius during the following periods:

20 January 1903 to 12 April 1905
17 August 1905 to 7 January 1906
24 February 1932 to 12 August 1932

20 November 1932 to 14 February 1935
4 January 1962 to 23 March 1964
17 September 1964 to 15 December 1964

A well-aspected Saturn in Aquarius can give a great deal of influence and prosperity, especially in government and other large organizations. You are well-known among a wide circle of friends and acquaintants, whatever your walk of life. If you were to become a public figure of importance, you would have great appeal for the masses. You can be recognized in the fields of music, either popular or classic, or like Bob Hope you can be an eminent humorist. You may also excel in literature or science, and there are no limits to the heights you can attain in politics.

You are more democratic than your friends with Saturn in Capricorn, but nevertheless you like to run things and have your own way. However, you are more subtle about getting it. Aquarius's influence on Saturn makes you less self-centred than is usual and you possess more understanding of the human condition. You realize your own true importance in proportion to the rest of the world, and while you can be autocratic, you are not bound up in your own ego.

You are a humanitarian first and foremost, with true insight into human nature and a belief in the brotherhood of man. This position gives real wisdom in maturity.

Saturn in Aquarius can cause accidents to the lower leg or ankles: the lymph glands may also give problems.

Famous people with Saturn in Aquarius:
Lord Byron   William Blake
Winston Churchill   Greta Garbo
Bing Crosby   Cary Grant
Elvis Presley

Saturn in Pisces

Saturn was in Pisces during the following periods:

12 April 1905 to 16 August 1905
7 January 1906 to 19 March 1908
15 February 1935 to 24 April 1937
17 October 1937 to 13 January 1938

24 March 1964 to 16 September 1964
16 December 1964 to 3 March 1967

This is a good position for gathering wisdom for the soul's eternal enlightenment. Pisces is the sign of sorrows and a planet as restricting as Saturn is not fortunate in a material sense. If afflicted, it is an indication of worldly misfortune; well-aspected, the harshness of Saturn is lessened and the egocentricity reduced. However, unless the planet is very well-aspected, there is disappointment over the position you may have to occupy in life. At some time your popularity will suffer, and if you are in an enviable position you can be attacked by both inferiors and equals. If in an inferior position, you may suffer at some stage through the animosity of superiors. Saturn in Pisces can cause others to try to detract from your good reputation, and you can suffer on this account.

Well-aspected, Saturn in Pisces gives a vivid imagination as well as great vision, which is a real asset for the creative scientist. With writers, poets or performers, there is a certain whimsical quality which adds charm. You may be fascinated by any writings or teachings that are tinged with mysticism and, given a favourable aspect, you may derive great solace from your chosen religion or from the study of astrology.

You are not inclined to be as self-centred and materialistic as is usual with Saturn, and life may demand from you more than an average amount of self-sacrifice. If Saturn is well-aspected, however, you have learnt to accept the conditions of your life philosophically.

You are especially susceptible to illness caused by impurities in the fluids of your system, and the most vulnerable part of your body is your feet.

Famous people with Saturn in Pisces:

Sir Isaac Newton	Julie Andrews
Henry Fonda	Warren Beatty
Françoise Sagan	Jane Fonda
Rex Harrison	John Wayne

Punters' Luck for 1988

Jockeys for the 1988 Flat Racing Season – Lucky Dates

Gambling is always a precarious business of course, and the following has been compiled in order to help the regular race-goer to minimize his losing bets.

The dates given are the good days shown on the jockey's birth chart.

WILLIE CARSON March 18th; April 6th (especially good), 10th, 11th and 18th; May 6th (especially good), 23rd (especially good), 26th; June 3rd, 19th, 22nd and 25th; August 5th–12th inclusive, 14th, 25th (especially good); September 1st (especially good), 9th, 25th (especially good); October 6th, 25th (especially good); November 1st (especially good), 7th–13th inclusive.

STEVE CAUTHEN March 14th–25th inclusive, 19th and 20th (both especially good); April 6th, 7th, 8th (especially good), 23rd (especially good); May 1st, 24th, 27th; June 3rd, 24th (especially good), 29th; July 3rd, 14th, 22nd and 27th; August 11th, 12th–16th inclusive, 13th and 14th (both especially good); September 2nd (especially good), 10th (especially good), 19th, 26th; October 7th (especially good), 14th, 26th, 29th (especially good), 30th, 31st; November 1st–8th inclusive (1st and 8th both especially good).

PAT EDDERY March 13th, 19th, 21st; April 2nd, 7th, 12th, 20th (especially good), 24th; May 2nd, 3rd (especially good), 8th, 9th, 27th, 28th; June 3rd (especially good), 10th (especially good), 11th, 19th, 21st; July 1st, 2nd, 5th, 10th, 17th, 25th, 26th (especially good); August – good month in general but the 4th, 5th and 9th especially good; September 5th, 7th, 15th (especially good), 26th; October 6th (especially good), 11th, 15th, 25th, 28th (especially good), 29th; November 5th, 7th–12th inclusive (11th especially good), 14th.

R. HILLS March 17th, 18th–31st inclusive, 21st, 23rd (especially good); April 6th, 15th, 22nd, 24th (especially good) (a good month in general); May 6th (especially good), 7th, 10th (especially good), 12th (especially good), 18th, 22nd, 24th, 31st; June 1st–4th inclusive, 12th, 22nd, 28th; July 6th, 7th, 17th (especially good), 23rd; August 3rd, 8th (especially good), 9th (especially good), 14th (especially good), 16th, 17th (especially good), 18th, 23rd, 24th; September 12th, 16th, 21st; October 3rd (especially good), 9th (especially good), 11th, 15th, 24th, 26th and 27th (both especially good); November 10th, 12th, 14th (especially good).

M. HILLS March 17th, 20th (especially good), 22nd (especially good), 28th, 31st; April 10th, 24th (especially good), 25th (especially good), 29th (especially good), 30th; May 6th (especially good), 9th (especially good), 11th (especially good), 14th (especially good), 18th; June 3rd (especially good), 7th (especially good), 12th (especially good), 21st, 22nd, 27th (especially good); July 2nd (especially good), 13th, 22nd (especially good), 26th (especially good), 28th; August 1st, 3rd, 15th, 17th (especially good), 18th, 21st, 23rd (especially good), 26th, 27th; September 1st, 8th, 9th, 13th, 17th, 23rd, 28th; October 14th, 16th, 17th, 21st and 27th; November 1st, 9th, 13th (especially good).

RICHARD QUINN March 28th (especially good), 31st; April 1st–3rd inclusive, 5th, 17th, 23rd, 27th, 28th (especially good); May 14th, 23rd, 29th and 31st (both especially good); June 1st (especially good), 5th, 6th (especially good), 21st, 28th, 29th (especially good) (in general a good month); July 1st–11th inclusive, 11th (especially good), 13th–17th inclusive, 18th (especially good), 30th; August 10th, 25th, 29th, 31st; September 3rd, 12th, 22nd (especially good), 30th (especially good); October 1st, 2nd (especially good), 13th, 19th, 20th; November 9th.

JOHN REID March 12th, 14th, 25th, 28th, 31st; April 1st, 3rd, 8th (especially good), 20th, 24th, 25th, 26th, 28th; May 3rd, 4th, 20th, 28th; June 22nd, 29th; July 8th, 19th, 20th, 27th (especially good), 28th; August 6th (especially good), 10th, 13th; September 5th, 7th, 16th, 27th; October 7th (especially good),

13th–15th inclusive, 16th, 21st, 24th, 29th; November 6th–14th inclusive.

P. ROBINSON March 22nd (especially good); April 6th, 9th (especially good), 15th, 26th (especially good); May 5th, 9th, 11th (especially good), 15th, 18th, 23rd, 29th; June 1st–4th inclusive, 10th, 16th–19th inclusive (16th especially good), 17th, 23rd, 24th, 30th; July 1st, 2nd, 11th (especially good), 12th, 23rd; August 7th (especially good), 12th, 18th, 24th, 28th (especially good); September 1st, 8th (especially good), 12th (especially good), 13th, 15th, 17th, 25th, 27th, 28th; October 9th, 10th, 12th, 13th, 15th (especially good), 21st, 28th, 29th; November 3rd, 8th.

BRIAN ROUSE March 16th, 20th (especially good); April 4th, 5th, 7th, 10th, 20th (especially good), 28th–30th inclusive; May 3rd–14th inclusive (4th and 5th especially good), 18th, 21st, 22nd, 23rd; June 1st–7th inclusive, 12th; July 2nd (especially good), 3rd, 14th, 15th, 23rd–26th inclusive, 28th; August 7th, 12th, 31st; September 7th (especially good), 14th, 21st, 23rd, 27th; October 4th, 16th–22nd inclusive (16th especially good), 23rd (especially good), 31st; November 4th, 5th, 6th, 7th, 8th.

WALTER SWINBURN March 20th, 24th (especially good), 27th (especially good), 28th; April 1st, 7th, 12th, 13th, 22nd, 24th; May 3rd, 8th, 12th, 16th, 29th (especially good); June 7th–22nd inclusive (a particularly good month with the 2nd, 6th, 8th and 9th all especially good); July 1st, 3rd, 15th, 23rd, 24th, 30th; August 2nd, 6th, 7th, 10th (especially good), 12th, 15th, 27th; September 2nd, 4th, 6th, 8th, 20th, 27th, 30th; October 1st, 2nd, 8th, 10th, 25th, 27th, 29th; November 2nd, 4th, 12th.

S. BARCLAY March 17th, 22nd, 24th, 31st; April 3rd, 7th, 8th, 12th, 16th, 25th; May 1st, 4th, 9th (especially good), 13th, 15th, 25th; June 4th, 7th, 8th, 13th, 24th, 25th, 29th; July 1st (especially good), 2nd, 3rd, 17th; August 6th, 10th, 11th, 15th, 17th; September 2nd, 4th, 10th, 15th (especially good), 26th, 27th; October 3rd, 4th (especially good), 16th, 18th, 26th, 27th; November 2nd, 6th, 7th.

N. CARLISLE March 18th (especially good), 20th, 31st (especially good); April 1st, 16th, 18th (especially good), 24th,

26th; May 2nd, 12th, 16th, 17th, 27th–30th inclusive (27th especially good); June 1st (especially good), 2nd, 5th, 6th, 14th, 15th, 17th, 19th; July 1st–3rd inclusive, 6th, 7th, 9th, 18th (especially good), 20th, 24th; August 2nd, 10th, 18th, 19th (especially good), 23rd, 28th, 29th; September 3rd (especially good), 17th, 19th, 21st, 24th; October 11th, 13th, 18th, 19th, 20th, 21st, 26th; November 4th, 7th (especially good), 12th.

Trainers for the 1988 Flat Racing Season – Lucky Dates

The following dates could be particularly useful when combined with those previously given for the jockeys.

CLIVE BRITTAIN March 21st, 29th; April 8th (especially good), 14th, 15th, 29th, 30th (especially good); May 1st, 2nd, 5th (especially good), 9th, 17th, 29th–31st inclusive; June 3rd, 4th, 16th, 17th (especially good), 18th, 22nd (especially good), 29th, 30th; July 2nd, 11th, 15th–20th inclusive (18th especially good), 22nd, 23rd (especially good); September 8th, 15th (especially good); October 10th and 12th (both especially good), 30th, 31st; November 1st–3rd inclusive, 14th.

GUY HARWOOD April 20th, 25th (especially good), 29th; May 7th, 10th, 14th, 23rd (especially good), 24th (especially good), 27th; June 8th, 9th (especially good), 11th, 12th (especially good), 19th (especially good), 20th, 21st, 26th (especially good) (20th–28th inclusive all good); July 2nd, 12th, 20th, 21st, 22nd (especially good), 26th; August 6th, 11th, 12th, 17th, 20th, 23rd; September 3rd, 4th, 11th (especially good), 12th (especially good), 14th, 24th, 28th; October 10th (especially good), 11th (especially good), 12th, 15th (especially good), 18th, 20th, 22nd, 26th, 28th, 29th (especially good); November 10th, 11th, 12th.

RICHARD HERN March 22nd–25th inclusive (22nd especially good); April 3rd, 4th, 5th (especially good), 17th, 19th (especially good), 22nd, 23rd, 28th (all in all a good month); May 4th, 8th, 15th, 17th, 18th, 20th, 21st, 22nd–28th inclusive (23rd, 24th, 27th and 28th especially good); June 1st, 4th, 5th, 8th, 12th, 20th, 24th; July 3rd, 7th (especially good), 13th, 14th, 19th, 22nd, 23rd, 25th, 29th; August 4th, 6th, 12th, 22nd, 26th, 30th; September 4th (especially good), 6th, 7th (especially good), 9th, 10th, 11th, 17th, 21st, 22nd, 23rd, 27th; October 4th, 5th, 16th, 22nd, 28th, 29th, 30th (especially good).

BARRY HILLS March 20th, 31st (especially good); April 1st, 2nd, 10th (especially good), 16th (especially good), 22nd (especially good), 25th (especially good), 27th, 28th (especially good); May 3rd, 4th, 25th, 30th; June 11th, 13th, 14th (especially good), 22nd, 26th, 29th; July 3rd, 12th, 17th, 19th, 25th, 27th, 28th; August 3rd, 12th, 13th (especially good), 15th (especially good), 25th, 28th (especially good), 29th, 31st; September 3rd (especially good), 12th, 17th, 18th, 26th, 27th, 28th; October 4th, 8th (especially good), 9th, 11th, 14th (especially good), 17th, 19th (especially good), 21st, 22nd, 28th; November 3rd (especially good), 5th (especially good).

MICHAEL ANDREW JARVIS March 18th, 20th, 22nd, 24th, 25th (especially good), 31st; April 1st, 2nd (especially good), 3rd, 6th, 7th, 9th (especially good), 22nd, 23rd; May 7th, 10th, 11th, 16th, 26th, 30th, 31st; June 1st, 11th, 17th, 20th, 26th (especially good), 29th; July 15th, 17th, 23rd, 25th, 26th, 28th (especially good), 31st; August 7th (especially good), 9th, 13th, 25th, 30th, 31st (especially good); September 1st–4th inclusive (3rd especially good), 5th, 12th, 20th (especially good), 23rd (especially good), 26th, 27th, 28th (especially good); October 10th, 12th–19th inclusive (15th especially good), 21st (especially good), 25th; November 3rd, 13th (both especially good).

FULKE JOHNSON-HOUGHTON March 17th, 20th; April 4th, 5th, 7th, 20th (especially good), 30th, May 5th, 21st, 22nd, 23rd, 26th–31st inclusive; June 1st–5th inclusive; July 14th, 15th (especially good), 23rd (especially good), 24th–26th inclusive, 28th, 29th; August 7th, 31st; September 7th (especially good), 14th, 23rd (especially good), 27th; October 15th, 21st, 23rd (especially good), 30th (especially good), 31st; November 6th, 7th, 9th, 10th.

DAVID O'BRIEN March 14th, 17th, 23rd (especially good), 27th–31st inclusive (29th especially good); April 3rd (especially good), 17th (especially good), 19th (especially good), 23rd (especially good); May 3rd, 9th, 10th, 18th (especially good), 25th, 27th, 30th; June 1st, 18th, 19th (especially good); July 8th (especially good), 9th (especially good), 20th (especially good),

21st (especially good), 26th (especially good), 29th (a great month in general), August 1st–14th inclusive (4th and 12th especially good), 20th (especially good); September 10th, 29th; October 1st–20th inclusive (2nd, 4th and 20th especially good), 26th (especially good); November 3rd, 5th (especially good).

GAVIN PRITCHARD GORDON March 13th, 16th (especially good), 24th, 26th, 28th, 31st; April 1st, 10th, 23rd, 24th (especially good), 25th–28th inclusive; May 1st, 2nd, 3rd, 4th, 8th, 11th, 27th, 29th; June 1st (especially good), 2nd (especially good), 7th (especially good), 8th, 9th, 18th, 27th, 29th; July 3rd (especially good), 6th, 7th, 10th, 15th (especially good), 19th, 31st; August 3rd (especially good), 4th, 9th, 18th–31st inclusive (19th especially good); September 1st–3rd inclusive, 4th, 5th, 7th, 8th, 9th, 15th, 17th (especially good), 29th (especially good); October 1st (especially good), 4th (especially good), 5th (especially good), 14th, 20th; November 1st, 3rd, 8th, 13th.

MICHAEL STOUTE March 17th, 19th, 20th, 24th, 27th, 28th, 29th; April 7th, 8th, 13th, 22nd, 23rd, 24th (especially good); May 7th, 13th–16th inclusive (16th especially good), 19th (especially good), 20th (especially good), 25th, 28th–31st inclusive (28th especially good); June 10th, 21st, 22nd, 25th (especially good), 29th; July 3rd, 15th, 18th, 19th, 26th (especially good), 27th (especially good), 30th (especially good); August 3rd, 11th, 12th, 15th, 19th–26th inclusive (20th especially good), 29th; September 1st, 2nd (especially good), 9th, 18th, 26th, 27th (especially good), 30th; October 1st (especially good), 3rd, 5th, 19th, 22nd (especially good), 24th–31st inclusive (29th especially good), November 2nd (especially good), 4th (especially good), 9th (especially good), 13th, 18th.

JOHN SUTCLIFFE March 17th, 18th (especially good), 19th, 21st, 22nd; April 5th (especially good), 9th, 10th, 21st, 22nd, 24th–30th inclusive; May 6th, 22nd, 23rd, 24th, 25th, 26th (especially good), 28th; June 10th, 12th–23rd inclusive, 27th, 28th; July 16th, 17th, 18th, 23rd–25th inclusive (24th especially good), 29th; August 5th, 8th, 9th, 12th, 13th, 18th, 24th, 25th; September 1st, 7th, 8th, 9th, 19th, 24th, 25th; October 4th, 5th, 6th, 8th–12th inclusive, 24th, 25th, 29th; November 7th, 8th, 11th, 12th.

JOHN FRANCOME March 17th, 21st, 23rd, 27th; April 5th, 8th, 12th, 22nd, 23rd (especially good), 30th; May 3rd, 6th, 17th, 24th; June 17th, 22nd, 24th; July 1st, 14th, 19th, 20th, 21st, 22nd, 25th, 30th; August 9th–17th inclusive (10th, 11th and 14th all especially good), 26th (especially good); September 2nd, 11th, 17th, 22nd (especially good), 23rd, 27th; October 1st, 4th, 8th, 14th, 28th–31st inclusive (29th especially good); November 1st–9th (1st, 7th both especially good).

Your Pets and Astrology

Aries 21 March to 20 April
On the credit side, your Aries pet will be affectionate, warm
and extremely loyal. However, an inability to learn from past
mistakes can lead to training problems and great patience is
therefore required in this respect. Healthwise, such an animal
is invariably accident-prone and physical safety is constantly
endangered by its own tendency towards haste and impulse. The
physical area most in jeopardy is the head. Keep a vigilant watch
on this part of the body. With this advice borne in mind, your
companion will lead a long, happy life.

Taurus 21 April to 21 May
No training problems here; the Taurean pet is naturally
obedient. The only exception is on occasions when the Taurean
stubbornness is rampant. Take your pet for a walk, throw a
stick for him to retrieve and for no obvious reason he will
suddenly sit down as if rooted to the spot, looking you up and
down as if to say, 'You fetch it, I'm simply not in the mood.'
The same applies to the feline of the species. 'Have you any
idea how stupid you look crawling around with that piece of
string?' her expression seems to say. Coax and cajole all you
like, but your Taurean pet won't budge when its mind is set
against doing so. But at least there is no problem where food is
concerned, for this animal loves to satiate itself. There is nothing
so content as a well-fed Taurean. However, do guard against
gluttony, for this could obviously undermine health.

Gemini 22 May to 21 June
The Geminian pet is pure joy – ever-ready for a game and with
a delightfully wicked sense of humour. This small animal refuses
to grow up, and at fifteen and even later will chase a ball just
as energetically as it did when a small kitten or puppy. This type
is very erratic and tends to eat when it wants to, with the result
that it is often a nibbler. Sleep and exercise are also taken
according to mood: one day lazy and constantly snoozing, to
the point where you suspect something must be wrong; and the

next zooming around like a maniac with no thought for rest at all. Because of this, owners need to keep an eye on food intake and exercise, for although this animal will never admit to it, Geminians do need the correct diet and exercise in order to stay healthy.

Cancer   22 June to 22 July
The Cancerian animal makes an excellent family pet. It takes a maternal interest in every single member of the family and can fret to the point of extreme when someone is absent. Whether feline or canine this animal loves water, especially if introduced to it at an early age. Furthermore, it has a sweet tooth, but before you allow your pet to indulge in left-over desserts or to nibble at bars of chocolate, bear in mind that those precious teeth have to last a long time. Therefore, unless you can train your pet to brush its teeth, you would be extremely unwise to encourage this side of its character. Healthwise the stomach is often delicate but quick to recuperate from any problems.

Leo   23 July to 23 August
This animal instinctively knows how to put most humans in their place. Never lose sight of the fact that you are dealing with royalty and as such the Leo type demands the respect it innately knows to be its right. Therefore, discourage children from dressing up the family pet; it will never forgive you and may pack a bundle in a spotted handkerchief and leave home! When training, play on the Achilles' heel of Leo subjects – namely a love of flattery. Constantly tell your pet how beautiful, brave, or clever he or she is and watch the response. You will no doubt bore your friends by relating tales of how your animal seems to know every word you say and so it does – especially when it comes to extolling his/her virtues. Healthwise, this type has two extremes: either never ill or else always on the sick list. Pay special attention to the back, for this is the Leo's vulnerable area.

Virgo   24 August to 23 Sept
If you are a slob then you would be very ill-advised to purchase a Virgoan pet, since your untidiness could cause a nervous breakdown. Drop a sock or stocking on the floor and you will experience a hot sensation at the back of the neck; turn round and you are faced with a pair of indignant, accusing eyes. Better

50

pick up the offending item at once! The Virgoan animal is fastidious both with food and physical cleanliness. Cranky food habits are expected and you will not change this, so accept it. Ideally this type makes a great pet for those living alone. It is intelligent, playful but somewhat nervous; therefore noisy children are difficult for it to accept. Healthwise, keep an alert eye open for skin and bowel problems.

Libra   24 Sept to 23 Oct

If you want an animal who will fit in with almost any situation, then this is your pet. Not because it is so adaptable, but more due to the fact that it is often too lazy to protest at any change. This therefore makes it an ideal family pet, but do ensure that children do not take advantage of its easygoing nature. Invariably this is an affectionate, sensible and devoted pet. Food presents little or no complications as this type devours anything; not surprisingly, in many cases this tendency can lead to a weight problem in later life. The Libran weak spot is the kidneys, so owners are advised to keep a wary eye open for any troubles in this direction and always ensure that your pet has easy access to fresh water. This will help to minimize health problems.

Scorpio   24 Oct to 22 Nov

If your pet loves you and is born under the sign of Scorpio, then you have complete devotion; but if for some reason you don't come up to scratch, then he or she will be off. Therefore you need to shape up before it's too late. Jealousy can also present you with a hazard. A new baby – or worse still, a new pet – will cause this kind to pine and liberal amounts of love will be needed if it is to accept the intruder. Maybe it never will do so, but at least an uneasy truce can be achieved if you know how to handle this particular type. Being a water subject, your pet will drink gallons of it and love to be in or near it. Therefore, no problems are expected when it comes to bathtime, quite the reverse. Such enthusiasm can lead to one hell of a mess and cover everything within a six-foot radius. Healthwise, the Scorpio rules the genitals and infections there are fairly common. Much depends on whether the animal is spayed or left intact. Not a pet for the faint-hearted.

Sagittarius   23 Nov to 21 Dec

This is the real sport of the zodiac, and the more fresh air and exercise the better – therefore not an ideal pet to own if you live in a poky flat or bedsitter. Such an animal would be most distressed in such circumstances. Besides, this has got to be the clumsiest animal ever, so that a small living area could spell nothing short of disaster. Furthermore, even those living in spacious houses should put delicate furniture well out of reach; this animal can't help it, no matter how much training it receives. The Sagittarian pet is an adaptable sort. It will accept new members of the family with glee and a move of house is regarded as a wild adventure – no pining for the old home here. A great family pet then, full of life and fun.

Capricorn   22 Dec to 20 January
This is the sign of the late developer, therefore owners must not fret if such an animal is slow to mature either physically or mentally. This type is a fighter, one who will put up with almost anything and remain loyal. It does possess one fault, however, and that is a tendency to snobbishness. No one is better than HIS FAMILY and visitors are viewed with disdain; this is especially applicable if your pet be feline. Foodwise there are no problems and in this particular area, discrimination flies out of the window. Furthermore the pet under this sign will be somewhat reserved; certainly it loves you but has no need to make a fool of itself when showing this. Healthwise, owners need to be watchful for dental problems, colds and accidents to the knees. But in the main, this is usually a healthy and long-lived specimen.

Aquarius   21 January to 19 February
This too can be the detached type. There will be times when a vacant look enters your pet's eyes and you may come to the conclusion that he or she is just plain stupid. Little do you realize that this animal has probably just worked out a chemical cure for some disease, or invented the first robot replica of itself for companionship's sake. Furthermore, this is the sign of the logical thinker, so don't try to con such an animal and never be condescending. This type has a great sense of fun, so Aquarian animals make excellent family pets. Healthwise, problems associated with the eyes or circulation should never be neglected, for these are the Aquarian's vulnerable areas.

Pisces   20 February to 20 March

This type can only be an ideal family pet where there are older children. Little tots can be so cruel and here it must be borne in mind that we are dealing with a most sensitive sign. Your pet will always be ready to be treated like a baby, with lots of attention and love. Obviously, then, a home which is frequently empty such as a bachelor pad would be most unsuitable; the animal might stray and would fret exceedingly. Physically the Pisces pet appears delicate and even fragile, when in actual fact the constitution can often match that of an ox. Be sure that food and drink are always fresh, since this could represent a health hazard. Bullying of any description is ill-advised and may actually cause illness. Training should be undertaken with a firm but gentle hand for the best results. Never lose sight of the fact that this animal wants to please; it is his/her mission in life, so don't be too hard on the Pisces pet.

Compatibilities

Two animals are frequently twice as much fun as one. But when choosing a companion for your pet, life can be made considerably easier if you select one of its astrological compatibles. See the list below.

Fire signs: Aries, Leo and Sagittarius (all compatible).
Water signs: Cancer, Scorpio, Pisces (all compatible).
Air signs: Gemini, Libra, Aquarius (all compatible).
Earth signs: Taurus, Virgo, Capricorn (all compatible).

Spaying or doctoring should not be undertaken when the moon is in the following signs: Scorpio, Libra, Virgo. During these periods, complications are likely to occur. Refer to the tables at the back of the book.

The Year in Focus

For you the most important part of the coming year will be from January until 7 March, for at this time Jupiter continues in your sign, throwing a rosy glow over all aspects of your life. Between these dates you will be protected from any real disappointment and harm; therefore it is imperative that you make all important moves now. Lady Luck will not be quite so sweet once this period has passed.

When Jupiter leaves your sign it enters Taurus during the second week in March, and although this affords you a certain amount of protection where finances and possessions are concerned, you would be most unwise to rely on chance in any other area of life.

From a professional standpoint, the year is particularly fortunate for those of you involved in travel, entertainment, politics and teaching. People connected with these professions could also influence your life quite considerably. For other Arians the placing of Saturn, Uranus and Neptune all at the zenith of your chart indicates a certain amount of confusion, disappointment and unexpected occurrences in connection with your work and status. Control the impulsive side to your character and think all schemes through to their logical end. Your tendency to take on five things at once and complete none of them would be the worst way to go during 1988.

On the romantic side, again it is the period between February and March which shines down upon you. Anyone new you meet during this time will be particularly fortunate for you and those who are planning on wedding bells or emotional commitments have chosen wisely.

Healthwise, apart from a certain amount of accident-proneness around November and December, you should be fighting fit.

The reins then are clearly in your hands during the year ahead, so it's up to you to take advantage of the good periods and tread ever-so-carefully during the more tricky times.

Now for a more in-depth look.

January

Hopefully you are not involved in any kind of long-distance travelling during this particular month. If you are this could be complicated, disappointing and in general a complete waste of time. Furthermore, should any foreigners enter your life or it be necessary to work alongside them, then you are advised to curb that impatient and sometimes aggressive side to your character, or feelings could be hurt all round. Romantically, up until the 15th friends will afford you the best opportunities for meeting interesting members of the opposite sex. After this date, you will develop a perverse preference for those committed elsewhere. Not surprisingly you are in danger of being your own worst enemy in this respect. If you are artistic, then it may be necessary to involve yourself in some extra research or simply take work home in order to catch up. But you will be positively inspired and at a later date others will appreciate your efforts.

In general, those from Australia or with connections in this country will be particularly fortunate for you. Golden opportunities await in this direction. Should it become necessary to sign any kind of document during this month, try to do so on the 26th or 27th. If in doubt, then for heaven's sake ask a solicitor to check over a contract or document for you. Financially speaking, friends will be full of ideas on how you can boost your sagging resources and some of these will be sound – at least up to the 15th. After this date, that small modicum of financial good sense which is yours seems to fly hopelessly out of the window. So curb extravagant impulses after mid-month. Healthwise, apart from an occasional problem in connection with over-indulgence you are in A1 condition.

February

The first week of the month is a somewhat frustrating one. People are reluctant to make commitments or take decisions, and this wreaks havoc with your nervous disposition. However, after the 10th when Venus enters your sign, the picture changes. You are mentally and physically in top form and other people fall over themselves both professionally and personally to help you. Any new romantic liaisons begun during this month will be particularly fortunate and important. Professional partnerships can also be instigated with a certain amount of success.

Socially, invitations positively pour in, although be warned that entertainment could prove more expensive than you envisaged. From the 10th onwards is a particularly fortunate time for the artistic Ram, and all can gain from combining business with pleasure on numerous occasions.

Mars enters the zenith of your chart on the 22nd: after this date, workload is increased quite considerably and all that splendid energy of yours will be required if you are to cope. The sports person enjoys a particularly lucky phase during the last ten days of February. Health in general for the month is good, although there will be times when your flow of energy suddenly deserts you; if you are wise, you will set aside some days for complete relaxation so as to avoid ending the month feeling like a wet dishcloth.

March

During this month your ruling planet rules the zenith of your chart in Capricorn. This places the emphasis on the ambitious side to your character, but there is a certain amount of stress and hard work shown; you will need all your splendid vitality if you are to cope. Not surprisingly there will be times when you suffer from exhaustion, so fit in some early nights. The lucky professions are those associated with uniformed occupations, sport, companies dealing with metals – precious or otherwise – and enterprise. The luckiest period from a romantic point of view is during the first week while Venus hovers in your sign. This is also an excellent time socially, when most of the enjoyment is likely to be crammed in. After this, life becomes rather quiet on a personal level. Financially, Venus' move into Taurus on the 6th shows money spent on beautifying either your surroundings or yourself. But do control extravagance where social life is concerned; you don't have to mortgage an arm and a leg in order to enjoy yourself – if you do, there is something wrong somewhere!

March is basically a month during which you should be independent. Other people, especially on the working front, could be quarrelsome and tense. Don't give them any reason for complaint. Healthwise you are fairly robust, but there will be one or two bouts of over-indulgence which will take its toll, also the occasional evening when you are suffering from complete and utter exhaustion; however, if you can overcome these two pitfalls, then it should be a fairly healthy month for you. Lastly, those involved in the money professions receive some interesting news.

April

The workaholic continues on the rampage until the 7th, when your ruler Mars moves into Aquarius and calms you down quite considerably. This is not to say you will not be busy in your professional capacity, but it does mean you may develop a slightly better sense of proportion. Mars' move into Aquarius occupies the friendship section of your birth chart, so much energy will be going out in this direction. Also you are likely to be roped in to organize some function in connection with a club. Furthermore, sporty types should be extremely fortunate during the months ahead. Romantically, Venus' move into Gemini on the 4th increases your chance of brief encounters whilst on short trips. And it is while in the throes of fulfilling your daily obligations, such as shopping, that you will meet interesting new members of the opposite sex; however, there is something impermanent about these relationships, so don't set too much store on them. Mercury enters your sign on the 6th and squats there until the 20th; while this placing will liven up your entire personality, basically it may make you somewhat nervous and easily upset on occasions. Many of you will be extremely restless during the month ahead and will fly to the travel agents in an effort to alleviate this. Any opportunity to travel should be snapped up, while those professionally involved in import, export, travel, foreigners, communications and the media should all enjoy a relatively good April.

With Saturn in close conjunction with Uranus at present, you should be particularly careful about what you say and do in front of superiors or older work colleagues. They could spring one or two nasty surprises. If you are a freelance worker, then you will be signing a contract approximately mid-month which should boost the coffers somewhat. Many of you will develop new interests during April, perhaps of an intellectual variety rather than purely physical. Financially, a big hole may be made in your resources by your inability to fight off the urge to own some much-coveted status symbol. If you can resist, do, but if not you should be prepared to pull in your belt another notch or two. An interesting month.

May

Professionally speaking it is a good time for those who are connected with the money professions – financiers, bankers, accountants etc. But all Ariens will be devoting a good deal of time and energy to friends until the 21st anyway. After this date, your ruler Mars moves into your solar twelfth house and you can become a good deal more reclusive and anti-social. Romantically it's not a startling month for games of Romeo and Juliet, although you continue to meet interesting people in the most unlikely places until the 17th. Social life is also hectic for the first three weeks, but after this you decide that home is the place for you; it's likely that many of you will be indulging in home improvements during the latter part of the month. If you are a younger reader with special favours to ask of parents, then strike during the first week; after this they are unlikely to appreciate or understand your side of the question. Healthwise, the first two weeks find you hale and hearty but after this you develop an unfortunate knack of picking up any stray microbe or germ which is running around. It won't take much to send your temperature soaring – and when that happens, for heaven's sake look after yourself. Lastly, when confronted with any kind of professional problem, bear in mind that you will find the answer somewhere in your past experience. There will be much going over old tracks during ensuing months.

June

This is a hectic month for those professionally involved with buying and selling, communications, publishing or transport. There may even be news of a rise or increased status during the month ahead. But you would be most unwise to sign any kind of contract or document before Mercury resumes forward action on the 25th; if you do, the chances are that you will have overlooked the small print, and that the document or contract is likely to be unlucky in some way. Venus in retrograde action is an indication that when it comes to romance and other people, you will have the unhappy knack of being in the wrong place at the wrong time. Take care what you put in writing, for this is open to misinterpretation. In this particular direction Ariens already committed are better off, but even here a yawning gap in communication is likely to appear. Try to be lighthearted and casual where emotions are concerned. Financially, if you are waiting for money in the mail I'm afraid you will have to carry on doing just that for some time. Finance arriving in this particular way is open to delay and complication. Clearly, then, it's going to be a tricky month, but if you watch out for the pitfalls you should emerge relatively unscathed.

July

On a professional level it is a particularly fortunate time for those involved in property and allied trades. If this applies to you, you can expect an increase in profits and some good news in connection with promotion. However, in the main most Arians will be in an anti-social and domestic mood. Family and home occupy you during the first couple of weeks; just for once you are happy with this state of affairs and will be disinclined to play the social butterfly. However, when Mars enters your sign on the 15th things change and you become more aggressive, vital, passionate and sexy. The latter part of the month is particularly fortunate for the professional sportsmen and those in uniformed occupations. Romance should be fun, although unimportant. Passions are easily aroused, although just as easily they die. Not a time, then, for meeting that special someone, but you can have a great deal of fun looking during July.

Healthwise, being accident-prone is likely after the 15th, for with Mars in your sign you will be vulnerable to dangers through hot and sharp objects, also sudden fevers and accidents caused by haste. You would also be well advised to keep an eye on food and drink intake: suspect food at the back of the fridge should be thrown out promptly. If eating out, do make sure the establishment comes up to the highest hygiene standards.

Financially speaking, long awaited cheques finally arrive and those of you attempting to sell possessions should be delighted by the prices you manage to achieve. If you have booked a holiday during this month, then for heaven's sake double-check all arrangements. The backward movement of Saturn and Uranus could lead to complication, loss and disappointment if you are not careful, so don't leave anything to chance. A very up-and-down month.

August

Mars continues to weave its way through your signs, leaving passions, emotions and senses all razor-sharp. All born under this sign will have abundant energy which must be channelled out positively, i.e. in sport. Otherwise you could deteriorate into irritability and aggression. Jupiter moves into Gemini, bringing good fortune for the next few months to those of you involved in communications, publishing and buying and selling. Financially, much money seems to be going out within the family on home decoration. Socializing will for the most part take place within the domestic environment and you will shine as a host or hostess. Mercury's move into Virgo on the 13th won't help your nerves and there will be times when those around will be extremely irritating. Try to spend your time with people who have a calming effect on you. If you are going on holiday, take precautions against thieves and don't take romance too seriously – simply have lighthearted fun.

September

Once more Mars continues in your sign, but right now it is in retrograde action and for every step you take forward, it will be necessary to take two back. This applies in all directions. There will be many occasions when you find yourself drifting back to the past and a yen to visit old places will be strong, although possibly disappointing if you succumb to it. If you are taking part in any kind of sport, be on your guard against sprains and strains. Generally speaking, on a physical level you must not push yourself too hard at this time, or there could be accidents and general well-being will suffer. On a professional level, it is a good month for those involved in any kind of work which provides a service. Increased productivity is also likely. With Mercury's move into your opposition having anything but a calming effect on your nerves, it tends to stir up restlessness in those around you too. Others will be difficult to pin down and it's not really the ideal time to ask for any kind of favour. But one of the high points of the month is your social life, for Venus' move into Leo brings you into contact with interesting, influential and exciting people, who extend invitations which should be accepted. Social life will provide many opportunities to meet members of the opposite sex, although it's unlikely that anything will actually develop during the month ahead. An interesting month.

October

October is invariably the month which is devoted to partnership. There is no point in being too headstrong and independent, because you need other people during this time and you may as well accept the fact. It is an excellent month for forming professional partnerships. They will be well-starred, but steer clear of signing any kind of contract in connection with the same until after the 21st. Socially, the first week is the best. Your only trouble will be in fulfilling all your obligations. Not surprisingly, such popularity will have a slightly adverse effect on your health if you give in to over-indulgent impulses. Armed forces and physical occupations suffer something of a set-back which begins to sort itself out after the 29th. Financially speaking, you would be most unwise to speculate in any direction. Stick to the budget and all will be well.

November

A good month for those dealing with or working in occupations connected with insurance, big business, banking etc. Not a time for any Arian to take chances with law-breaking – if you do, you are sure to pay the price! Venus continues in Libra for the greater part of the month, so love-life is greatly enhanced up to the 25th. Those of you in existing relationships will find them deepening and becoming warmer; better understanding will be reached between you and your opposite number. Now that Mars has resumed forward action, it is a good time for all kinds of physical work and sports in particular. Healthwise, although there is an inclination to be accident-prone for the most part you are hale and hearty although tending to excitability and emotional behaviour. Financially you are likely to gain through the ideas of other people, so keep your eyes and ears wide open.

December

Those of you waiting for news from abroad, or from foreigners, should receive it during the first two weeks of this month. It is also an excellent time for those involved with teaching and higher education in particular. Emotionally there is a certain amount of discord early in the month, but as December wears on the romantic undertones surface and emotional commitments are likely for many. Financially speaking, your affairs seem tied up with other people, which should work out well in the long run. If you are able to get away this Christmas, then this would be ideal. The further you can escape from the home front, the happier you will be. With Venus and Mars both in fire signs, it is likely to be something of a memorable Christmas for you and the year should end on a satisfactory note.

Day-by-day Horoscope

January

1st – You are likely to continue with merry-making for some time, but it is unlikely that partners wish to follow suit. You will therefore have quite a frustrating day. Friends may be agreeable; call them up.

2nd – Make the most of opportunities that come your way, be they social or business. This is a good day for mixing, and any invitations which allow you to do this should be accepted without a second thought.

3rd – This is the beginning of a go-ahead period and you are advised to make the most of prevailing conditions. Today is a good time for getting superiors and work colleagues on your side.

4th – You will have to inform partners of your ambitions, so as to allow yourself freedom of movement. This afternoon is an excellent time for contacting those who have been useful to you in the past.

5th – Do not allow the grass to grow under your feet. There are some excellent opportunities for advancement which you will have to be quick to seize on.

6th – You will add success to an improvement in income today. The backing which an older colleague gives you will make all the difference.

7th – Those working at home will be pleasantly surprised by the results. All forms of teamwork will be well-rewarded. Others out and about will be feeling restless, as if they are wasting time.

8th – Duty calls must be made today, as you are unlikely to get round to them for some time to come. Relatives will be pleased to see you this evening, but could take advantage of your good nature.

9th – What is important to you today is not so much how you feel as what you are accomplishing. Other people may be slowing you down and you will have to have words with them.

10th – Try not to upset too many people with your ambitious attitude. Keep things in proportion. Partners may be complaining of neglect this evening.

11th – You will be experiencing a greater urge for independence in your work, and consultations with superiors are becoming necessary.

12th – Those travelling in the course of their business will have a successful day, provided they are aggressive in their approach to contacts. Do not be put off by procrastination on the part of another.

13th – A good day for getting what you want from others. You will not be able to put a foot wrong so long as your approach is right. This evening is a favourable time for getting friends and colleagues together.

14th – Check your post this morning, as there will be an important letter you are likely to overlook. Financial gains are likely for those willing to take a few risks.

15th – Children will be giving parents a hard time today and will need to be put firmly in their place. Do not allow anyone to dictate the day's events: make your plans and stick to them.

16th – A good day for applying for a rise in salary, although it would be advisable to steer clear of asking for promotion just yet. That will come later in the month.

17th – You will be on the look-out for ways to improve your working conditions, and you are on the right track. Consult workmates for opinions if you are meeting them socially.

18th – Social matters have an effect on your career. Superiors are easily approached today and they will answer any queries you put to them.

19th – Allow other people to lead the way, as you will learn a lot from their behaviour. This afternoon is likely to be a time of frustration, since things are not moving as swiftly as you would wish.

20th – Financial gains are likely for those who have had cash at risk for some time. Dividends are likely to be higher than anticipated.

21st – A good day for getting out and about. Physical contacts and sports will appeal, as will all physical pursuits. Heavy jobs that need your attention on the whole will be attacked with gusto.

22nd – A fairly quiet day, so you can conserve some of your energy. You will need periods of rest and relaxation if you are to continue at your present rate.

23rd – A period of discretion is needed owing to the fact that a project has not really taken off as you had hoped. Don't give in; try to get out. It will lighten your mood.

24th – Those seeking promotion can put the feelers out tomorrow. In the meantime, do try to relax and rest those tattered nerves.

25th – Changes of policy in your place of employment may put you down the list for promotion candidates. You will have to be content to mark time with your plans – make a move when the aspects are more favourable.

26th – Those who are married will be reaching greater understanding where your ambitions are concerned, but the single will have a lot of explaining to do.

27th – Not the best day of the month for personal relationships. You will find yourself at loggerheads with someone you consider a very close friend. Be tactful and use diplomacy if differences of opinion arise.

28th – Flirtatious behaviour on the part of married Ariens will lead to upsets with partners. Be sensible when dealing with attractive members of the opposite sex.

29th – Relations are complaining of neglect, so you will have to make some courtesy calls to set their minds at rest. Do not allow friends to pay for your entertainment today; you will have difficulty in repaying them.

30th – Today is full of surprises. Someone you have hitherto regarded as a rival will make their true colours known.

31st – Dealing with officialdom in its many guises will probably leave you short of finance. Those in positions of power and authority are about to get their pound of flesh and there is little you can do about it.

February

1st – A good start to the month, when news of a salary rise reaches you. Those working from home will have a financial offer to consider.

2nd – Someone you have not expected to see for some time makes an appearance and you will be delighted. An unexpected gift will also come your way.

3rd – Push yourself forward today so that others can see your talents and abilities. It is not a day for taking a back seat. The unemployed attending interviews will achieve more by using tact rather than aggression.

4th – A day which ideally should be spent in the company of those who stimulate you on an intellectual level. This is not the time for physical endeavour.

5th – Home entertaining is especially successful today. Try to mix business with pleasure. Superiors will be willing to visit you in your home.

6th – Minor health problems will affect you today and along with a moody partner, this could be something of a bad day.

7th – A good day for laying down long-term plans. You will need to explain your actions to other people, so that they do not feel insecure.

8th – Do not allow others to dictate the pace of the day. Set yourself a target and work towards it steadily. The afternoon is the best time for dealing with contacts who are distant.

9th – Financially you are likely to make some gains and some losses. Care should be taken when spending cash on essential items, as you are likely to be taken for a ride.

10th – A good day for all those travelling in the course of their business. A new contact can be made who will be important to you in the future. This evening is the best time for getting together with superiors.

11th – Today should ideally be spent away from home. If this is not possible you will have to make do with what entertainment you make for yourself, and this could be expensive.

12th – Try to get loved ones to see your point of view when differences of opinion arise. Arguments are inevitable, but need not be too angry.

13th – If you are involved in a job that requires attention to detail, effort and concentration, then you are in for a good day. Your intuition and judgement are very well tuned and you will see through many people.

14th – A favourable day for gamblers; Lady Luck appears to be on your side. People with cash at risk will hear of good dividends. This afternoon is an excellent time for becoming involved with the ideas of another person.

15th – Those working from home will be subject to interruption and delay, and there is nothing to be done about it. Make the most of the time available to you.

16th – Many of you will begin to feel the pressure of a greater-than-average work-load. Delegate wherever possible, or you will have to take work home.

17th – Anything that has to be channelled through official sources can be pushed through quickly. But take care you do not overlook tiny details; otherwise you will have officials breathing down your neck.

18th – Those involved with organizing sporting fixtures will have an excellent day, as will spectators. Participants will find bruises and strains hard to avoid.

19th – A quiet day when you will be free of interruption. Now is the time for you to get together with partners and make some plans for the future.

20th – You will probably have to change your opinions about a workmate. Do not let this come as shock to you. This is a day when many people will be surprising you by their actions.

21st – Changes will have to be made in your routine in order for you to get through the day unscathed. What at first seems simple will become more complicated as you become involved in it.

22nd – You could be reacting too violently to what others say to you. Try to keep your temper under control. Your emotions will be bared this evening when a loved one upsets you.

23rd – Possibly you could be making some silly mistakes, and these will be costly in terms of both finance and time.

24th – You will be doing things on the spur of the moment today, so will have to remain flexible. Do not make any hard and fast decisions, for they will have to be changed at the last minute.

25th – Something of an element of doubt crops up with younger people today. Their ideals may not match your own, but at least they will be more sound.

26th – A loved one is trying to force your hand over a domestic matter. Do not allow this to occur. Married Ariens should not let their emotions get out of hand when dealing with members of the opposite sex.

27th – A good day for making plans, but not for putting them into operation. Consultations about your career will have to wait until after the weekend.

28th – Older friends have some good advice for you and you are advised to act on it. Financial losses are indicated this afternoon for housewives out shopping.

29th – This month goes out on a high note. You will have more energy than of late and will be able to deal with jobs that much quicker. Routine work is cleared away early and a new, more challenging task is begun.

March

1st – Minor health problems are receding and you will be feeling more like getting things done. Do not allow other people to stand in your way

2nd – Householders are advised to be on their guard against doorstep salesmen with so-called bargains for sale. Money spent on essential items will not be wasted. Parents will find children demanding this evening.

3rd – A good day for dealing with neglected tasks in and around the house. Catch up on correspondence and telephone calls. This afternoon is a good time for entertaining in your own home.

4th – There is an urge to change your surroundings for the better and any work done to this end will provide satisfaction. House-owners will be intent on redecoration and plans for this should be made.

5th – Try to settle into a routine at work. Plan your day methodically so as to get the most out of it. Any time wasted now is likely to cost you money. Romance is probable for the single.

6th – Those connected with the arts and entertainment will receive some interesting news. In fact, in all areas you are advised to pay extra attention to your mail.

7th – Not good news if you are romantically inclined. A relationship begun some time ago will crash about your ears. Be philosophical and do not grasp at straws.

8th – Do not try to sort out legal problems today: your judgement is faulty and you will make some expensive mistakes. Those trying to sell their homes will have a bit of luck this afternoon.

9th – A good time for handling paperwork of any description. Routine matters could also prove to be of value.

10th – Romance bites the dust today in no uncertain terms, and a relationship you thought indestructible falls by the wayside.

11th – Housewives are warned to be on their guard against con-men and unscrupulous salespeople. When making purchases, change should be checked every time.

12th – Changes you make in your arrangements will cause others to be angry with you. Try to stick to plans wherever possible.

13th – Not a good day for working about the home. Minor accidents are likely, especially if working with hot or sharp objects.

14th – A good day if you are trying to get a new scheme or project off the ground. Workmates will be helpful and cooperative, but do not tax their patience.

15th – This is a time when you should be laying down long-term plans both in your professional life and your career. Keep your eyes on workmates if you wish to learn something to your advantage.

16th – Those making journeys today will find their arrangements going haywire. Double-check all aspects of travel. Those working from home should have a very productive time.

17th – Not a good day for investing jointly-owned finances, but there is nothing against putting your own cash at risk, however.

18th – If you are in need of financial assistance or advice, go to see your accountant or bank manager this morning. Legal documents should not be signed this afternoon.

19th – Those involved with sports are somewhat accident-prone. Sprains, strains and bruises are likely. Try to avoid physical contacts.

20th – A fairly quiet day when nothing should interfere with your leisure time. Go ahead and do whatever you want. This evening should ideally be spent with relatives.

21st – Your ambitions surface today and you will be in a go-ahead frame of mind. Do not allow anyone to stand in your way. If approaching superiors, do so with confidence.

22nd – Arguments and confrontations abound. Guard your tongue and then later you will regret nothing you have said. This evening will be quieter. Kiss and make up.

23rd – Relatives are able to give you the right sort of advice in connection with your career. Workmates will set you on the right trail should you turn to them.

24th – You should not allow yourself to be guided by your head. You are in danger of following schemes which have little or no chance of success.

25th – Make certain that your goals are attainable. You are in danger of putting a lot of effort into things which are unimportant. You are not sure of yourself, so stick to routine.

26th – Get away out of the house today, as much as you can – preferably on your own. You will not be much company this weekend, so don't put relationships at risk.

27th – Pay attention to what older people tell you. You could learn from their past mistakes as well as your own. Family and friends will delight in your company.

28th – If putting off any business transactions which are under way, you would be advised to make certain that you are dealing with trustworthy people.

29th – Do not overtax your energy today. Headaches and other minor stressful problems are likely. Pace yourself and do not worry others with your problems.

30th – Do not become involved with matters that do not directly affect you, especially the problems of other people.

31st – A good day to put long-term plans into operation, and for clearing up the debris of your working life. Any one of these matters should be dealt with early in the day.

April

1st – It might be April Fools' Day, but you are not about to be taken for a ride by anyone. You certainly have your wits about you, and in fact manage to stay one step ahead of everyone in most respects.

2nd – The full Moon in your opposition warns you to handle your relationships with care. Circumstances are changing and something could very well come to an end.

3rd – The a.m. hours are the best time for trying to extract favours. After this, forget it and be self-sufficient.

4th – The Moon meets up with Pluto this afternoon and so you will be in a restless and vulnerable mood. This evening, increased popularity leads to many new invitations.

5th – There will be little time for enjoying yourself today – those around will be pushing you along. Workload will be heavier. As a result, you need to plan yourself an easy evening.

6th – Keep expenditure down. You are likely to experience a series of impulses which you will live to regret, so think twice before bargain-hunting.

7th – Yesterday's advice still stands. Stick to that budget of yours. Romantically you feel in a flirtatious mood, and you may find this difficult to handle.

8th – A good time for the professional sales-person or the bargain-hunter. A short trip is likely this evening in order to visit family.

9th – You may be flighty, but you find it difficult to switch off work. Loved ones are likely to complain. Get well away from the domestic front in order to relax.

10th – Calls on friends or relatives should be left until the afternoon, as your presence will not be appreciated during the morning. If you are single, there may be interesting encounters with members of the opposite sex this evening.

11th – An excellent day for those of you who work within a small group of people. Club affairs are well-starred, especially if they are to do with sport. A new objective is likely.

12th – Get to grips with important issues early. Some time after three o'clock, concentration begins to wane and you become more anti-social. A quiet evening is likely.

13th – Domestic and property affairs may be causing you something of a headache, and this is likely to curtail your social activities. An excellent evening for taking work home in order to catch up.

14th – You are still in a somewhat anti-social mood until the afternoon, when you blossom out and come into your own. You will then be pushing ahead with work, in particular making social arrangements. A good day for those involved in research.

15th – You may find you are a real power-house at the moment and you accomplish more today than perhaps during the rest of the week. Keep plenty of energy in reserve for this evening.

16th – The new Moon in your sign affects domestic and property affairs. Therefore an excellent day for house-hunting or making domestic changes. Romantically, you will get your own way, so push ahead.

17th – Romance is hard to discover and even harder to hang on to. Single people may find that a cosy relationship is heading for a bumpy ride. Marrieds could find partners somewhat boring.

18th – In any business where you have to present a good image to the public, you should do extremely well today. However, confidence may run out in a couple of days and you should not procrastinate in any direction.

19th – Your head is buzzing with various ideas, so make notes – some of them will prove to be worthwhile. Short trips are well-starred. There is some interesting news regarding relatives.

20th – A very hectic day. In order to take advantage of all the opportunities that are coming your way, you will need to get yourself organized – but make plans before you move.

21st – The emphasis is on property affairs. You may therefore find this a good day to approach elders for favours. Many of you will be planning home improvements, so budget sensibly.

22nd – If you have engaged anyone to make improvements on your home, you will need to make adjustments to your working day so as to cope. This is an excellent time for house-hunting.

23rd – Initially, the day may look as if it is going to be boring, but at approximately 5 o'clock the rest of the world remembers you exist and invitations pour in. Don't take life too seriously: attractions will be purely sexual.

24th – If you are married, this is an excellent day for getting out with the children. It will be less of a hassle than usual and the kids will be in a good mood. The evening is a good time for pursuing a romantic affair with members of the opposite sex.

25th – You are likely to return to work with something of a hangover today after your hectic weekend. Therefore attend to routine work and shelve anything of major importance. Try to plan a relaxing evening.

26th – You will be on the move for most of the day and this will be extremely tiring. Those at work should be tactful with workmates. Petty jealousies and enemies could cause trouble.

27th – Someone at home may not be in A1 condition and you should not demand extra time or energy from them.

28th – Things are difficult to handle until 4 o'clock: therefore don't try! After this time, though, others are willing to be supportive, and are interested in your opinion. An excellent evening for discussions with loved ones.

29th – Other people make you feel important and needed. The only problem is that they are somewhat changeable and while only too willing to make commitments, it is likely that they will have to withdraw their support at a later date.

30th – Those close to you are likely to be enjoying the limelight. If you are single a new romance is likely, but don't get yourself too deeply involved.

May

1st – Try to avoid socializing with workmates, as things could go horribly wrong. Also you may be feeling a little exhausted. If so, put your feet up in front of the TV and don't be afraid to explain to friends how you feel.

2nd – Those on the work scene are the bearers of news – some of it good, some of it fabricated, so don't take it too seriously. Sportsmen are likely to find themselves drained of energy.

3rd – Don't do anything important until after lunch. With the Moon entering your fire sign you will be your usual dominating, vital and enthusiastic self. Don't be too idealistic where romantic affairs are concerned.

4th – A good day for those involved in the teaching profession or higher education. Money seems to be coming and going rather quickly, so do be careful.

5th – If you need to present ideas to other people, then do so before lunch, or they will not be prepared to listen. The next couple of weeks are excellent for those of you involved in selling, advertising or the media.

6th – Property and home affairs dominate. If you are a housewife you can be assured of a steady stream of visitors, so make sure you have plenty of food and drink around.

7th – Not a madly exciting day. It would be better to potter around the house rather than do anything too adventurous. Someone may try to enlist your help in connection with a club; leave your decision until tomorrow.

8th – Affairs, friendships and clubs all dominate. It should be an interesting day and one during which you will meet plenty of new people. Good for romance.

9th – Your mood is on the lighter side of life, i.e. socializing or romance. Someone you met over the weekend sets you thinking.

10th – Your intentions are generally positive, but this flies out of the window today and you seem unable to make decisions. So perhaps you shouldn't try. The day is a bit jittery – relax this evening.

11th – Still not at your sparkling best, unless you are involved in any kind of research. It is a time to use your instincts when it comes to making any decisions.

12th – The Moon in your sign stirs up all those fine Arian characteristics and no one can get the better of you. Do be warned against arguing for the sake of doing so. Popularity and confidence are on the upsurge.

13th – Expenses provide something of a headache. Sit down with your partner and see if you can sort them out. There is no point in avoiding those brown envelopes – they may need your attention.

14th – A good day for those involved in single contact sports.

Things at home will go well and this evening is an extremely good time for home entertaining.

15th – An active day when you will be out and about away from the home environment. Many of you will also be thinking of ways to beautify your surroundings and add value to your property.

16th – Yesterday's mood is likely to provide you with the opportunity to increase earnings, so keep your eyes and ears open. This evening a short trip will be particularly enjoyable.

17th – A new acquisition is likely, either a purchase or a gift. Those involved in advertising are likely to hear some exciting news.

18th – Any decision-making should be made before lunch, likewise any short trips. The rest of the time you are likely to be somewhat housebound, waiting for either deliveries or workmen. A quiet evening.

19th – Parents are likely to get in touch with you, although this may not be well received. Make sure you don't hurt their feelings.

20th – An excellent time for home entertaining, especially if you are hoping to impress someone of influence. Also a good day for pushing property affairs through.

21st – This is one of those weekends when you are determined to get the most out of everything. Romance, sport, affairs related to children are all well aspected. Get yourself organized.

22nd – A good time basically for having fun. Leave any romantic decisions and don't tackle them before tomorrow.

23rd – Now that Venus is in retrograde action, you could be less cooperative and romantic affairs might get horribly complicated. Perhaps it would be better if you could manage to remain a free agent. Workload is extra heavy.

24th – If your work provides any kind of service, then you are in for a progressive day. Should you intend to extract favours from bosses or supervisors, you will be disappointed.

25th – Rather a routine time, in fact a downright boring day. It is up to you to extend invitations and liven up your surroundings.

26th – New people enter your life in both working hours and leisure. If you are launching into one of those mad affairs of yours, make sure you leave your rose-tinted spectacles at home!

27th – People around are somewhat changeable, so weekend arrangements may be in a state of flux – something guaranteed to irritate the Arien.

28th – You are in a sensitive mood, and if you are on your own you will feel it acutely. Therefore make sure you have plenty of company.

29th – Discharge obligations to others; it is time to clear the board. Do not get involved in any hare-brained or 'under the counter' transactions.

30th – The third day when nothing appears to be making progress. The housewife will find herself with time on her hands. Why not slip down to the beauty salon or hairdresser?

31st – Another day when you will have plenty of time to put, your feet up. Workmates will also be kicking their heels. Make the most of this breathing space – try to come up with a cash-making idea.

June

1st – You can make money from travel, foreigners or sales. Romantically, a brief encounter could develop into something more interesting.

2nd – Those professionally involved with property and allied trades will be in for a productive time. Venus continuing in retrograde action complicates romance and financial affairs.

3rd – If travelling, ensure you have carefully made all arrangements, especially if roads are to be your method of transport. That car of yours may need some attention.

4th – Friends ask you to spend your leisure time with them, and if you are wise you will accept, as you are in a gregarious mood. Romantic affairs seem to be causing you a certain amount of heartache and this state of affairs is likely to go on for quite a while.

5th – If you go visiting today, then stay away from relatives. Their company will be somewhat depressing, so stick to close friends. Sporting affairs are well-starred.

6th – You are in an anti-social and reflective mood. When it comes to solving romantic or financial problems, use past experience – you will find it invaluable.

7th – Don't try to force the pace where other people are concerned. Persuasion will serve you far better than force.

8th – The Moon in your sign stirs up your sensitivity. You will be easily influenced by flattery and deeply hurt by criticism. Try to be a little more resilient today.

9th – You are so popular right now that you will have to start early with your weekend arrangements. Get yourself organized and lead life to the fullest extent during this period. Those of you who are unemployed could do well at interviews.

10th – You are likely to be greatly relieved because it is the end of the working week. If you are in the financial professions, then you will receive some good news.

11th – It is likely that you may have arranged some fairly ambitious plans which could drain your resources. You can impress other people without breaking the bank.

12th – You may be reluctant to stray very far until late afternoon, then quite suddenly your mood changes and you are likely to be more adventurous. Hopefully your opposite number can cope with you.

13th – Give and take a little today in order to get what you want. Financial gains will be made by those in the buying/selling industries.

14th – A good day for listening to the opinions of others. Bear this in mind if you are to change entertainment plans. A family problem will come to a head this afternoon.

15th – The new Moon in Cancer today starts the beginning of a new cycle in connection with property and domestic affairs. Many of you will be moving in the very near future.

16th – A good time for home entertaining. There may be some surprise news. Answer all telephone messages.

17th – Pay attention to what is going on around you and remain flexible at all times. You will have to change direction at some point during the day, so make certain this is to your advantage.

18th – Happiness will be added to your life, probably in the form of a new friend or relationship. Family celebrations look likely this evening – news about a birth or wedding, perhaps.

19th – You begin the day full of ideas on how to entertain yourself and your family. Better get out early though; enthusiasm seems to die off in late afternoon.

20th – Those making special preparations at home will see the successful completion of their efforts. Others will find that a business transaction is brought to a rewarding conclusion.

21st – Though a minor health problem could show itself today, you have no cause for alarm – your health is generally very good at present. Allow yourself periods of rest and relaxation throughout the day.

22nd – Once the Sun has well and truly entered Cancer, you begin a four-week period when the domestic and family side to life will dominate your waking hours. An above-average number of visitors can be expected in the near future.

23rd – An excellent day for acquiring the cooperation of other people, so don't be afraid to ask for it. Still a rather difficult time for romance, though.

24th – A splendid day for pleasing yourself. Those around you will not be making the usual demands on your time. Also a good time for beginning a course of self-improvement, dieting etc.

25th – Now that Mercury has resumed forward action, it is a good time for getting in contact with relatives. Also a much improved time from now on for those involved with sales.

26th – Those about to set out on a long journey may have to rearrange itineraries at the last moment. Be prepared for delays. Others will find a blocking influence in all they attempt.

27th – Mercury's forward action now makes it a lucky time for signing contracts or documents of all descriptions. A good day for attending to paper-work.

28th – Although it's true that the romantic side of your life may be going through a sticky patch, you are not making it any easier by being so idealistic.

29th – The full Moon in Capricorn today points to the end of a minor cycle in connection with work. Adjustments will have to be made. If entertaining, combine business with pleasure.

30th – Avoid making any financial decisions until the end of next week. Your money planet Venus is in retrograde action and things could become horribly complicated.

July

1st – Your ruling planet Mars in Pisces somewhat calms you down. Now and for the next few days, you adopt the strange role of shrinking violet, so don't be surprised if those around you are confused.

2nd – Be content to take part in what others have arranged, even if this goes against your own ideas. Now is not the time for taking the initiative. It would be best to let those around you take the lead in all areas of life.

3rd – You could be forgiven for wondering if someone has slipped you some 'ugly' pills. Life is rather quiet now, and is likely to remain so until later in the week unless you yourself make some arrangements.

4th – Some of your time could be taken up in planning and preparing the way for a new project. Those at home may be thinking about redecoration or a complete change of surroundings.

5th – At long last Venus has decided to resume forward action and from now on your relationships, both professional and personal, should be plain sailing. Also, the Moon in your sign after lunch increases confidence and popularity.

6th – A good day for the creative or artistic Arien, as sensitivity is heightened. However, do make certain you spend your time with those whose company you find congenial.

7th – You seem to have got your finances in something of a muddle (so what's new?), but if things look too serious, then seek the advice of professionals.

8th – Not a time for putting your talents or yourself on display. Your confidence is at a low ebb just now, but don't worry – it will be restored to you during the next few days.

9th – It is a routine day at home and work, therefore you will need to plan something this evening in order to stave off boredom.

10th – Get as far away from the home front as possible. A visit to a distant relative could be particularly successful. Romantically, take care you are not involved with someone already committed elsewhere.

11th – The full Moon in Gemini indicates that a relative of yours may be reaching an important decision which might affect you indirectly. Also, check out the car. It's not a day for taking chances in this direction.

12th – Mercury's move into Cancer is likely to stir up activity on the home front during the next few weeks. It is also a good time for handling property affairs.

13th – If you are entertaining, especially work colleagues, you will play the role of host or hostess successfully. Home improvements should be budgeted carefully.

14th – Your ruling planet Mars finally enters your own sign. The shrinking violet disappears and in its place you find Attila the Hun or Boadicea. You are bursting with confidence and enthusiasm, but please don't bulldoze others.

15th – An extremely fortunate time for the artistic or creative Arian. A financial offer is likely. Also exciting news for those who work with children or animals.

16th – Those born during the early part of the Arien period are somewhat accident-prone. All born under this sign are in an impulsive and impatient mood and life could become unbelievably complicated.

17th – You will need to take a firm line with relatives who are trying to offload their responsibilities on to you. You would do better to spend your social time with friends.

18th – This may not be the most exciting day of the year, but at least it will contain few problems. You should have much time on your hands, so put it to good use wherever possible.

19th – Don't expect cooperation from anyone around until at least mid-afternoon. Your best course up to then is one of self-sufficiency.

20th – Other people are difficult to pin down and you are in danger of attempting to apply that Arien force. Don't bother – it won't work. You will simply have to be patient.

21st – Things seem to be slipping somewhat today and your health is beginning to upset you slightly. But don't worry, it won't be anything serious.

22nd – Watch your food and drink intake – your stomach is rather easily upset at present. Also guard against minor accidents with hot or sharp objects. Younger people have an effect on the day's happenings and you will be changing your opinions for the better.

23rd – If you are a sportsman/sportswoman, then you are in for a successful, though somewhat accident-prone day. Don't take any chances. Romantically, brief encounters will be important.

24th – An excellent time for travelling and being adventurous, although when in the company of strangers you should curb aggressive impulses.

25th – Be content to take part in what others have arranged. Even if this goes against your own plans, it will be best to let them take the lead for a change rather than keep imposing your own ideas.

26th – A good day for combining business with pleasure wherever possible. Superiors are open to new ideas and invitations. Those hunting for a job could have some good luck.

27th – One of those accident-prone days again, so don't take chances, control impulsiveness. A busy day at work, with changes in the offing.

28th – Although some in authority will be happy to listen to your ideas and views, don't be too pushy. Use persuasion – it will serve you better.

29th – A day when friends and friendships are emphasized. Your social life looks as if it is going to pick up over the next couple of weeks.

30th – An excellent day for starting a holiday. Arrangements will go relatively smoothly, but be a little more flexible when dealing with foreigners.

31st – This is a splendid day for romance, so push your luck as hard as you can. If you are a woman, don't stand there holding a torch for someone – make your presence felt.

August

1st – Passions will be very easily touched during the month ahead, but avoid making commitments if you can, as fires may quickly die.

2nd – If travelling this morning, then guard against accidents. Furthermore, when leaving your home make sure it is secure. Confidence runs high today: there is little you cannot achieve if you put your mind to it.

3rd – Your confident mood continues and you bounce through life adding vitality and enthusiasm to other people's existence. An excellent day for sportsmen.

4th – If entertaining today, don't push the boat out in order to impress, just be your usual sweet and vital Arian self.

5th – There is likely to be an opportunity to bring in some extra cash. Keep your eyes and ears open in order to take advantage. Some interesting invitations for you – you are unlikely to be short of activity this week.

6th – Those participating in sporting events are in danger of minor accidents, sprains and bruises. Others will discover that arrangements may go astray unless they are double-checked.

7th – A good day for dealing with bureaucracy, officialdom and those in authority. If you were born during the last week of the Arien period, this is an excellent time for you.

8th – Financial good fortune is likely, but you won't know unless you push your luck and take a few minor chances. An unexpected gift is also likely.

9th – A new relationship formed today will be particularly fortunate, be it professional or personal. Marrieds will be enjoying a time full of fun and excitement.

10th – The emphasis is on matters connected with education, travel or foreigners. Your mood is one of idealism, but don't take this too far.

11th – If you desire to buy or sell something important, then act immediately. After the 16th transactions of this kind could go wrong.

12th – Although it's a weekend, you find it hard to shake off work and its problems. A quiet word with your mate may help in this direction.

13th – Plan a quiet Saturday. If you have relatives calling, try to rearrange things. You will be feeling tired and not in the mood for chatting. An early night is advised.

14th – You will enjoy the company of some close friends or neighbours, but don't be too adventurous – you are not at your most lively. A chat with a loved one could be productive.

15th – If there are any doubts about the sincerity of a workmate or friend, then do without their help. Complications will set in where other people are not as committed as you yourself.

16th – You are not at your most sociable at present, not with the Moon where it is today. Keep to daily routine.

17th – Don't plan anything romantic today, it just isn't the right time. It is much better to stick to what you know. Stay at home tonight.

18th – A good time for dealing with any Scorpions that may be in your life. Plan a get-together with friends this evening.

19th – Make sure that any new plans or projects have the support of superiors. Going it alone is ill-advised, so enlist the help of those around you. Bargain-hunters will find articles far away from their usual shopping location.

20th – Mars in your sign continues to provide a surge of confidence and you begin a four-week period when you can push ahead with self-interest of all kinds.

21st – Back to work with relish! You have new ideas and plans you wish to put to others, and these should be well received. The housewife can tackle work with one hand tied behind her back and still have time to visit friends.

22nd – You will be playing a supporting role with regard to the ideas and plans of friends and/or loved ones. Go along with whatever they have in mind, as their ideas are better than yours at present.

23rd – All relationships should be blooming. If you are thinking of marrying in the next couple of weeks, you have chosen an ideal time. Finances, too, seem to gain through partnerships.

24th – Members of the opposite sex will have an important part to play in the day's events. You could pick up some useful information from them. Extra cash is indicated.

25th – A good day for routine matters, but not for starting anything new. Jobs which require concentration and effort should be avoided, as the stakes are loaded against you.

26th – A member of the family could be giving you a hard time. Try to discover what you are supposed to have done. This afternoon is the best time to seek others' opinions.

27th – Today favours anything connected with entertainment and travel. It is a good time for getting away from the home environment and hunting down places of interest.

28th – Minor accidents are likely for those working with sharp or hot instruments – also for Ariens operating complicated machinery. Extra care should be taken by all today.

29th – Restlessness could set in today. Do not make plans for your leisure hours. Friends will have some excellent ideas, but it is doubtful whether you are in the mood to take their lead.

30th – You will be at your best during daylight hours. However, as time goes on you become more restless and nervous, not to say irritable. Therefore, if you are wise you will stay at home this evening rather than inflicting yourself on other people.

31st – Your irritable mood continues until after lunch, when you begin to feel human once more. Visit friends or neighhbours this evening; it will be enjoyable. Financial good fortune is indicated.

September

1st – Make the most of today – it is excellent for pushing all matters of self-interest. Good for the uniformed occupations and sports, and for making any kind of progress in life.

2nd – Your ruler Mars goes into backward movement for approximately seven weeks. From now on you will find that in taking one step forward, you'll also be taking two steps back.

3rd – You will be straining at the leash today, but those around you will not be of like mind. You will have to go it alone, or else remain restless and frustrated throughout the day.

4th – Peace will reign in domestic life, although there is some kind of confrontation with children. Today is also good for those hunting down jobs.

5th – Not a good time for making decisions where career matters are concerned. You will be feeling restless, but you should grin and bear things for the moment.

6th – The emphasis is mostly on the home; today is good for entertaining, improvement and generally getting together with the family. Contracts signed in professional partnerships will be lucky.

7th – It may be mid-week, but you are in the mood to enjoy yourself and are about to let everybody know. It is an excellent time for those involved in the arts and occupations connected with animals and children.

8th – Now that Venus is in Leo, be advised that you will fall in and out of love at the drop of a hat. It could be all good clean fun, but don't make any commitments for the time being. A lucky day for the artistic.

9th – Professional life springs problems, and you could be pushed to fulfil all professional engagements. Afternoon is the best time for important decisions.

10th – Don't stray too far away from the home today, as travel aspects are not that good. Any journeys you have to undertake should be kept to a minimum.

11th – Not a good day for visiting friends or relatives, so confine your trips to your own neighbourhood. This evening is an excellent time for home entertaining.

12th – You may be in a positive mood, but those around you are restless, refusing to be pinned down or to make decisions. The best tack to adopt is one of self-sufficiency.

13th – If you are single, there is likely to be someone new entering your life today. When leaving your home, make sure it is secure. Also, you are somewhat accident-prone.

14th – You will have difficulty in sitting still at all today – you are up and running all the time. The question is, where to? Do get yourself organized.

15th – Cash that was loaned out some time ago will be difficult to recoup, unless a concerted effort is made now. Many of you may find you suffer a small loss.

16th – Circumstances beyond your control make it necessary for you to change plans at the last minute. Fall in with whatever is on offer – you will have no choice.

17th – It's going to be a family day, with only one pitfall – namely, minor health hazards caused through over-indulgence. However, you may decide the fun is worth the price you have to pay. Certainly a good day for romance.

18th – The activity continues, although today's aspects tend to favour travel or sport. Both will be extremely lucky for you. Romantically, other people are difficult to understand.

19th – Problems that you may have with workmates should be sorted out as soon as possible. You may have to make one or two concessions in order to clear the air.

20th – Those with investments will find it necessary to review them and make whatever changes may be advisable. Expenses within the home should be watched carefully.

21st – Do keep active today, otherwise you will become irritable and be difficult to please. Partners will not be too cooperative where matters of entertainment are concerned this evening.

22nd – Whether at home or away, you will not be feeling much like joining in with others today. This is a time to seek out your own personal enjoyment.

23rd – You may not be too happy with what is going on around you, but you can rest assured that it will turn out for the best. Younger people make ideal companions this evening.

24th – Things pick up a little workwise, but there seems to be a black cloud descending slowly. You won't notice it too much other than being somewhat irritable. But this evening your mood appears to lighten.

25th – The full Moon in Pisces brings the end of a minor cycle for those involved in research. For other Ariens it is a depressing and moody day.

26th – There will be many discussions about finance today, both in your career and in your domestic situation. Career matters are helped along the way from an unexpected source.

27th – It is a good day for those in the entertainment industry. A contract or financial reward will come your way. Others will find it easy to avoid extravagance.

28th – If involved in any kind of sporting activity, you should take good care of yourself as minor accidents are likely. The same goes for those working in or around the house.

29th – A good day for making courtesy calls. Friends who have recently moved from your district should be contacted. Invitations from those younger than yourself should be accepted.

30th – You will need to be on your guard today against workmates who are out to interfere with your work. Delays and disappointments are likely for those who ignore advice.

October

1st – You may have to postpone a trip due to the behaviour of loved ones. News will be difficult to understand, but you should do your best.

2nd – It's true that partnership problems will arise, but you will be able to overcome them with tact and diplomacy. Financial matters will have to be watched carefully.

3rd – Wherever possible, avoid signing important documents for at least a couple of weeks – otherwise they will be unlucky for you. Short trips should also be avoided for the time being.

4th – Don't make any important decisions today, since your judgement is not at its best. Partners will be cooperative this evening, but do not ask too much of them.

5th – Although it is an excellent day for the creative and the sporting Arien, you should avoid committing yourself to any agreement for the time being.

6th – A good day for handling the affairs of offspring. Also, visits to friends and relatives will be successful. For the single, this evening is the best time for romance.

7th – You will have some breathing space today, so make the most of the time on your hands. A good day for planning for the future, especially in your domestic life.

8th – It looks as if someone you met some time ago is giving you a helping hand. Financial gains are likely this afternoon: be prepared to take small risks.

9th – If you want to have your way today, you will need to get it before lunchtime! After this, other people will become restless and indecisive.

10th – The day of the new Moon, and it falls in Libra. For you, this is likely to mean the beginning of a new relationship or fresh circumstances in an existing one.

11th – You will be feeling more optimistic, especially where domestic matters are concerned. Attend to routine matters early in the day, as they will become more complicated later on.

12th – Those working in and around the home will come up against unforeseen problems. Do not attempt to salvage mistakes, but call in a professional. This evening is a bad time for marrieds.

13th – Stay at home today; it will be best not to visit friends or relatives, as they will be in cantankerous mood. Conflicts are also likely between children and parents.

14th – Today is a time to look, listen and learn. You could find something to your advantage by listening to the conversation of others. Those working from home will have good news.

15th – Relationships begun today will not have much of a chance, so it's advisable not to pin your hopes on them. The single could find romance, but it will be short-lived. Try to resolve a family problem.

16th – Those pushing for a break in romantic affairs will have their hopes dashed. It appears that someone is deliberately blocking your progress and you will need to sort out things in a hurry.

17th – Do not be in too much of a hurry today, but plod on steadily towards your goal. Finances don't look too good, and you could have a small loss. Children will give parents a hard time.

18th – Use your intuition and initiative today. Opportunities for you to make progress are there, but you will need to have your wits about you if you are to benefit.

19th – Someone new enters your life. This encourages you to fresh initiative and a reappraisal of your objectives.

20th – A good time for completing jobs in and around the home. Joint ventures are best starred, so enlist the help of friends and family wherever necessary.

21st – If your job is connected with a service, then you can expect a progressive day and a certain amount of popularity. For others, workmates seem to be taking their share of the glory. You will have to be content to play a supporting role.

22nd – Not a good time for those working from home or on a freelance basis. Financial losses are indicated through carelessness and undue haste. Plan your day carefully.

23rd – Care should be taken by those travelling in the course of enjoyment. Minor accidents are likely. Also, housewives experience minor health problems.

24th – Stick to routine work today. Although better than yesterday, this is still not the most brilliant day for you. Unwind this evening and go to see friends: they will reassure you.

25th – The full Moon in the financial area of your chart indicates an end to a minor cycle in connection with finance. For some this will mean the end of a problem, but for the unlucky, it could be a dried-up source.

26th – Plan a quiet day, as you won't be feeling up to much.

Partners will for once be cooperative. Housewives are advised to take extra care when working in the kitchen.

27th – A good day for making calls on relatives. You will find the company of close family relaxing. This afternoon is also a good time for catching up on personal correspondence, paperwork and telephone calls.

28th – Let other people take the lead today. Your judgement is rather cloudy and you are in danger of making mistakes. Housewives are warned against buying items from unknown tradespeople.

29th – Routine matters are coped with easily and you will be looking for something more challenging to occupy your mind. Workmates and/or friends will be giving your confidence a boost.

30th – Minor health problems could ruin an otherwise good day. Domestic difficulties appear to be fading, thus taking a weight off your mind. Plan your day so that you clear routine matters early.

31st – Workmates and those around you will be more obliging than they have been for some time. You will find there has been some ill-feeling which has been dogging you at work.

November

1st – You won't have much time to spare this morning, and important decisions should be left until this afternoon. Try to mix business with pleasure – it will be lucky for you.

2nd – Partnerships with those younger than yourself will be particularly successful during the next week. Offspring delight you with a surprise (maybe they actually do their homework unaided!).

3rd – Do not ignore the warning signals being given out by your body. All minor health problems should be sorted out now and dental and medical checks are advised.

4th – A good day for putting long-term plans into operation with the assistance of superiors and workmates. You should be shooting for promotion now, so push ahead. Entertainment plans may need alteration at the last minute due to the indisposition of a partner.

5th – The ill-health of a partner or friend will still be affecting entertainment plans. Make alternative arrangements which are agreeable to all concerned.

6th – A quiet Sunday when you can give yourself some time. An excellent day for looking back over past mistakes and problems and learning a few lessons. Partners are on form this evening.

7th – Those working at home could have some good news this morning and housewives are advised to shop for bargains early in the day. A small financial gain is likely.

8th – An excellent time for those dealing directly with the public. Financial gains are shown. Those travelling in the course of their jobs should have some good news this afternoon.

9th – Not a day to spend on your home base. Get out and about in the company of friends wherever possible. Younger people make the best companions: they will stimulate and amuse.

10th – Any insecurities at work which you may have felt yesterday should be swept out of the way today. Other people are still not dependable, but you feel less threatened by them.

11th – Romance could come from an unexpected source for the unattached. A workmate will be the object of your desire. Marrieds will have to work hard to avoid frustration setting in.

12th – All teamwork and joint affairs should run smoothly, although you may have to pander to the erratic opinions of others. Family matters are beginning to sort themselves out.

13th – Give a thought to what others are saying about you at present – you could be the centre of some totally unfounded gossip. Partners will need convincing.

14th – A backlash from yesterday will still be in the air, but as the day progresses the situation will improve. If you did your homework properly with a partner last night, today should present little difficulty.

15th – Do not deliberately antagonize those around you, as you could bite off more than you can chew. You may receive some good advice from a friend, but you are unlikely to take it.

16th – Venus in your opposition should be throwing a peaceful veil over all relationships, especially the romantic. An excellent time for making emotional commitments.

17th – The rest of the month is an excellent period for those involved in the uniformed occupations, sport or anything which requires hard physical work.

18th – A good day for getting things done with regard to work or relationships. You could sort out a few problems if you use your intuition to full advantage. Financial gains are likely.

19th – Another day when finances could receive a boost – this time from an unexpected source. Watch others at work and try to pick up some tips. You could benefit from keeping your eyes open.

20th – The Moon in your sign means that you are likely to enjoy increased popularity and be in the limelight in your locale. You will be in demand.

21st – Not a good day for pushing things through official channels; best wait until a more favourable time. Those having problems with officialdom could find matters becoming worse.

22nd – A nose-to-the-grindstone sort of day, I'm afraid. However, bear in mind that good work done now will greatly benefit you in the months to come.

23rd – Those who have been waiting for cash to arrive could have a surprise – a cheque in the mail! Good news is in the air for those working in the communications areas.

24th – Invite friends or relatives into your home today, as this is a good time for a get-together. Romance is likely for the single.

25th – Do not waste your time and energy on things that do not concern you personally. Friends may seek your advice.

26th – Routine matters will become complicated if ignored. Clear up all work which has been neglected as you will need time to attempt something more challenging.

27th – Minor accidents are likely so take care of yourself, especially if handling hot or sharp objects.

28th – Take care in traffic. Also you will find that superiors are difficult and demanding and workmates deliberately perverse.

29th – Make certain that you have attended to all outstanding jobs before knocking off for the day. This evening is a time for letting your hair down and relaxing.

30th – Spend today relaxing and gathering your strength. This is not a good day for attempting work in the home. Relatives make good company this evening.

December

1st – Minor accidents will spoil your day and make things difficult for those around you. Arians who are travelling are especially at risk. Observe all traffic regulations.

2nd – Do not enter into joint financial gambles: also, keep expenditure to a minimum. This afternoon is the best time for making phone calls.

3rd – Those connected with the financial world will find things becoming difficult if they insist on working today. The afternoon and evening should be spent in the company of friends.

4th – Anything you are tackling around the home will be prone to interruption and interference. Housewives are advised against making do-it-yourself repairs to failed appliances – leave it to the professionals.

5th – Give older workmates the benefit of the doubt today, or you could find yourself in some difficult situations. Conflict is more than just a probability.

6th – Allow other people to take the limelight; it will be better to remain in the shadows for a while longer. Make long-term plans and be ready to put them into operation quite soon.

7th – A good day for family affairs. Problems will be solved due to the intervention of a relative. Marrieds will find their relationships becoming smoother, with less conflict.

8th – Not a day for falling in love, rather a time for consolidating what you already have. The single will need to give and take if they wish a relationship to blossom.

9th – A good day for hunting for bargains. The further you get from your home base, the better. Commercial travellers and representatives will find new contacts.

10th – The prospect of all that daunting Christmas shopping is bothering you. You should get someone to help you over the coming weekend, no matter how awful they think it is!

11th – Make all your courtesy calls today, as far as possible. You are in good spirits and this applies equally to those you visit. The evening is an excellent time for family get-togethers.

12th – Good work will be rewarded and many of you can expect windfalls. There is an air of optimism surrounding you at present, also plenty of invitations are pouring in.

13th – Festive and seasonal shopping can be completed today by those with an eye for a bargain. Housewives are advised to check their change, as losses are indicated in this direction.

14th – Wait until after the coming weekend before committing yourself to a partnership gamble. Do not, however, become involved in harebrained schemes or under-the-counter deals.

15th – If attending boozy functions at the office or factory, then make sure you don't use the car. Otherwise the combination of drink and driving could be disastrous.

16th – Partners and close associates will expect you to be at their beck and call. Although you find them demanding, go along with them – it will be to your advantage in the long term.

17th – Do not allow yourself to become complacent – you need to work for what you desire most. Help could come, from an unexpected quarter, and from the opposite sex.

18th – Finances will take a beating today and partners will want to know why. Try to control expenditure as much as possible. This evening is an excellent time for making personal plans.

19th – Minor health problems will loom in the form of headaches, eye-strain and hangovers. This is not the best day to attempt jobs that require concentration and attention to detail.

20th – Workmates are going to have a good deal of influence over the day's events and you will finish the day feeling resentful. Partners will not be as understanding as you had hoped.

21st – Not a good day for last-minute Christmas shopping. Housewives will be frustrated in their attempts to find bargains. However, this evening is an excellent time for partying, so accept all invitations.

22nd – If you are a male reader, do yourself a favour and get your Christmas shopping done now. Emergencies at work could mean that present-hunting will be out of the question at a later date. Control yourself whilst attending parties.

23rd – An excellent day for tracking down the superior who has been elusive for some time. Also for asking favours from those you admire.

24th – Parents will not surprisingly find children difficult to manage. Try to bear the time of year in mind. It's a very good day for getting together with close friends and neighbours. Try to get to bed at a reasonable time.

25th – HAPPY CHRISTMAS! There seems to be nothing to mar your day, although there is the likelihood of over-indulgence. Christmas spent with friends will be more successful than if spent with relatives.

26th – A party-going kind of day; you'll find much more amusement and entertainment with other people.

27th – Those at work will find workmates in a happy-go-lucky mood and erratic in their behaviour. Work will need to be double-checked.

28th – The single will find a big romance. Someone special is likely to walk into your life and remain there for a long time to come. A good day for friendship and love.

29th – Don't try to cram too much into the day or you could end up like a worn-out dishcloth. However, you may find it necessary to pay a visit to an elderly relative which will take up much of your time.

30th – You will have money on your mind and will be feeling depressed at your own extravagance. Those looking for romance find it this evening, but don't put too much emphasis on new relationships.

31st – An excellent day for putting yourself to rights; you will be in top form and others will take to you. If attending parties, make certain that you are in full control of your faculties, otherwise accidents are likely. HAPPY NEW YEAR!

The Moon and Your Moods

Our moods are clearly affected by the moon. After all, why on earth should such a well-balanced person as yourself be, on certain days, bad tempered, nervy, emotional, frigid and sentimental? Well, I'm afraid it is all down to the man in the moon. Prove it for yourself. Take a look at the moon table, then put it away for a month. In the meantime make notes of your moods, then rescue the table and you will notice a clear pattern of behaviour. You don't need an astrologer to work out for you that, during the month whilst you were making notes, the moon was in Scorpio when you were feeling depressed, in Cancer when you were feeling romantic, in Aries when you were bad tempered, etc. Your own individual pattern will be repeated each month; but do not be surprised if you are unaffected when the moon passes through, for example, Aries or Libra. Such a happening would merely indicate that these two signs are not particularly prominent on your birth chart.

Female readers would probably like to take a note of the fact that their menstrual cycle, if normal length, will begin when the moon is in the same sign each month. Why not have a try? You could find out a lot about yourself.

Moon Tables and Your Mood 1988

Jan	Feb	Mar	Apr	May	June	July	Aug	Sept	Oct	Nov	Dec	
												1
												2
												3
												4
												5
												6
												7
												8
												9
												10
												11
												12
												13
												14
												15
												16
												17
												18
												19
												20
												21
												22
												23
												24
												25
												26
												27
												28
												29
												30
												31

Legend:

- Aries
- Taurus
- Gemini
- Cancer
- Leo
- Virgo
- Libra
- Scorpio
- Sagittarius
- Capricorn
- Aquarius
- Pisces

Full and New Moons 1988

January	4th full in	♋
	19th new in	♑
February	2nd full in	♌
	17th new in	♒
March	3rd full in	♍
	18th new in	♓
April	2nd full in	♎
	16th new in	♈
May	1st full in	♏
	15th new in	♉
	31st full in	♐
June	7th new in	♊
	29th full in	♐
July	13th new in	♋
	29th full in	♒
August	12th new in	♌
	27th full in	♓
September	11th new in	♍
	25th full in	♓
October	10th new in	♎
	25th full in	♉
November	9th new in	♏
	23rd full in	♊
December	9th new in	♐
	23rd full in	♋

Key

🐏 Aries
🐂 Taurus
♊ Gemini
♋ Cancer

♌ Leo
♍ Virgo
♎ Libra
🦂 Scorpio

↗ Sagittarius
♑ Capricorn
♒ Aquarius
♓ Pisces